Truth, *Deception*
& God's Unfolding Purpose

**Midnight is Coming – God's Plan is Sure.
What do Truth and Deception Look Like
as the Age Draws to a Close?**

Phil Enlow

Revival Waves of Glory
BOOKS & PUBLISHING

Litchfield, IL 62056

© 2014 by Phil Enlow.

www.midnightcry.org

All rights reserved. No part of this book may be reproduced, stored in a retrieval system or transmitted in any form or by any means without the prior written permission of the publishers, except by a reviewer who may quote brief passages in a review to be printed in a newspaper, magazine or journal.

First Printing

Revival Waves of Glory Books & Publishing has allowed this work to remain exactly as the author intended, verbatim, without editorial input.

Scriptures taken from the Holy Bible, New International Version®, NIV®. Copyright © 1973, 1978, 1984 by Biblica, Inc.™ Used by permission of Zondervan. All rights reserved worldwide. www.zondervan.com The "NIV" and "New International Version" are trademarks registered in the United States Patent and Trademark Office by Biblica, Inc.™

PUBLISHED BY REVIVAL WAVES OF GLORY BOOKS & PUBLISHING
www.revivalwavesofgloryministries.com
Litchfield, IL

Preface

Suppose you are the devil. Go with me on this. You have been at war with the Most High God for a long time. Despite some mysterious promises made to a few who still serve Him you reign as god of this world. The overwhelming majority of its inhabitants remain firmly in your grip, cut off from their Creator, helpless in the hands of your forces who use and abuse them in gratifying their godless appetites. All is going according to plan.

Suddenly . . . a new development: God's own Son comes to earth. Yet he does not come as a mighty conqueror but as a tiny helpless baby. What a stroke of luck! What an opportunity to win it all and end the war with heaven!

But it's not that easy. Herod is stirred up to kill the young king as a potential threat but somehow he escapes. He grows up in relative obscurity but then is baptized by that rabble-rouser, John the Baptist. He goes to the desert to fast and pray and you seize the opportunity to dangle every temptation you can think of before him — but he stands firm.

He escapes every plot until — finally — over three years later you bring the jealous religious leaders and a compromised disciple together in a plot to get rid of him once and for all. You vent all of your fury against him, moving men to kill him in the most humiliating, painful way known among men. He dies and his tomb is sealed. Celebration time!

But three days later celebration turns to panic as Jesus rises, conquering death itself. Even worse, he is now alive with a life that cannot die. After a few weeks in which he appears to his followers he ascends to heaven itself — and there is nothing you can do to stop it. It starts to sink in: the war has been lost and you are on the losing side. A way out — provided by God Himself — has been opened so that your victims may escape and live in His kingdom forever — a kingdom from which you are forever shut out.

What do you do? Well, for sure you want to hide the good news from as many as possible but that doesn't work for everyone. Deception! That's what you are best at. After all, you invented it! And so you begin to devise every imaginable counterfeit designed to sidetrack people, causing them to miss out while believing that everything is OK. You become a master promoter of "Christian" religion. Anything is OK as long as people miss Christ and the sure salvation he provides.

Now imagine you are someone in today's world, bewildered by the array of religion claiming to represent Christ. It can't all be right. How can you tell? What does deception look like?

Introduction

The seed that has grown into this little book was planted in my heart several years ago during an overseas trip. Bro. Jimmy Robbins and I were ministering in a Pastors' Conference. It was our habit not to plan everything out but rather to wait on the Lord for His quickening and direction. Sometimes that came ahead of time and sometimes very close to the actual time for ministry.

That evening Bro. Jimmy felt led to minister on "Deception." He focused on several specific deceptions, ones known to our audience, exposing them in the light of God's Word. As he spoke the Lord began to quicken thoughts to me. One thought was that one could never keep up with all of the specific deceptions abroad in religion today. Not only are there too many but new ones are continually arising. As the age draws nearer and nearer to the end the devil is holding nothing back in his war against God. As he is a liar and the father of lies (John 8:44) deceit is his chief weapon.

The thought came distinctly to me that, as proper as it was to expose specific current areas of deception, God's people needed to be better equipped to recognize deception no matter what new form it might take. Satan is very clever at packaging his lies so that they appear to be truth. However, everything he does flows from his evil nature, producing a spiritual "flavor" that discerning followers of Jesus should be able to recognize.

That particular evening my thoughts centered on the spirit of deception expressed through religious leaders and so I shared a number of thoughts the Lord gave me from 1 Peter 5. I believe the Lord's blessing and witness were evident.

From that beginning I began to write and as I did the subject continued to unfold. Every time it appeared that the end was in sight another area of truth would open up, needing to be explored. And so this book seeks, rather than simply to lay out a "catalog" of deceivers and movements, to explore the **characteristics** of deception, to answer the question, "What does deception look like?" Whatever the details may be, when Satan is behind something it inevitably has a different look and feel than true biblical Christianity. John refers to the "Spirit of truth and the spirit of falsehood." 1 John 4:6. What God's people need is help in telling the difference. You might encounter a brand new form of deception but if you can recognize the spirit behind it you will be OK.

Of course, in addressing the total subject it is also necessary and proper to explore the parallel subject, "What Does Truth Look Like?" And so, much of the book seeks to answer that question in order that, in the light of truth, deception might be the more apparent.

Also, as the subject unfolded, I felt it needful to consider God's revealed purpose as the age draws nearer and nearer to a close. As a result of Satan's ongoing efforts many true believers have been put to sleep, they have been misdirected in their thinking and expectation, and they have been divided one from another.

In attempting to set forth characteristics of truth and deception I am aware that in some cases basically good men have been influenced by religious tradition and may exhibit some of the characteristics of deception, at least in a measure. In such cases there is a real need to honestly seek God, trusting Him to shed light as it is needed. He is willing and able.

Chapter 1

Agents of Deception

One does not need to be a Bible scholar to know that the scriptures contain many warnings about spiritual deception. For example, Peter, in 2 Peter 2:1-3 warns, "… there will be false teachers among you. They will secretly introduce destructive heresies, even denying the sovereign Lord who bought them — bringing swift destruction on themselves. Many will follow their shameful ways and will bring the way of truth into disrepute. In their greed these teachers will exploit you with stories they have made up."

As Paul the apostle was bidding the Ephesian elders goodbye for the last time he said, "I know that after I leave, savage wolves will come in among you and will not spare the flock. Even from your own number men will arise and distort the truth in order to draw away disciples after them. So be on your guard!" Acts 20:29-31.

1 Tim. 4:1 says, "The Spirit clearly says that in later times some will abandon the faith and follow deceiving spirits and things taught by demons." 2 Tim. 4:3 warns, "For the time will come when men will not put up with sound doctrine. Instead, to suit their own desires, they will gather around them a great number of teachers to say what their itching ears want to hear."

In fact this deception was to be so great that Jesus specially warned his disciples about it lest *they* be deceived. Jesus was shortly to go to the cross. He had just spoken to them about the Jewish temple being destroyed. And so in Matt. 24:3 we see the disciples come to Jesus privately to ask him some questions. "'Tell us,' they said, 'when will this happen, and what will be the sign of your coming and of the end of the age?'"

Please note that the answer Jesus gives is not directed at the world but rather at his followers: "Watch out that no one deceives you." The world is already deceived. Rev. 12:9. In 2 Cor. 4:4-5 we read, "The god of this age has blinded the minds of unbelievers, so that they cannot see the light of the gospel of the glory of Christ, who is the image of God." They are already prisoners of spiritual darkness. Rather, Jesus warned of deception that specially targets believers in order to lead them astray.

Matt. 24:5 continues, "For many will come in my name, claiming, 'I am the Christ,' and will deceive many." The agents of this deception were to be people coming in Christ's name, that is, they will claim to be sent by Christ, having heaven's authority behind what they say and do.

A very few of these will actually claim to *be* Christ, or God's Son, or something equally blasphemous. From time to time we hear news stories about some fringe group whose members blindly follow someone making that kind of claim. The fact that people will actually follow someone like that shows the condition they are in. When the one and only Jesus Christ returns there will be no doubt. Everyone will know it.

Of course, at that point it will be too late for anyone who is not ready. Matt. 24:30, 44, Luke 17:26-30.

Most deceivers will not go to such extremes, however. The word "Christ" simply means "an anointed one" and that is what they will claim to be. They present themselves as those sent of God. They cloak themselves in a mantle of supposed divine authority and proceed with their evil work.

Such men actually do have an "anointing" that inspires what they do. They have an ability to attract followers that goes beyond the natural. This ability comes from the master deceiver himself, Satan. Even though they may not be aware of it, they are actually servants of Satan and not the Christ they claim.

Satan's Rebellion

In the beginning Satan rebelled against his Maker, leading a third of the angels into his rebellion. The truth is, his rebellion was itself founded on deception — self-deception! Somehow he convinced himself that he could actually succeed in rising up against the Most High. I believe it is a mark of deception that every agent of deception is himself deceived as was the case with Satan. As 2 Tim. 3:13 says, "… evil men and impostors will go from bad to worse, deceiving and being deceived."

Satan continued his rebellion by seducing our first parents, Adam and Eve, into rebelling against God and the result is that mankind as a whole has been swallowed up by the terrible darkness of sin and death ever since. Sin reigns and judgment is coming. And that darkness is expressed not only in what we think of as gross wickedness, but also in religion that masquerades as righteousness.

Into this terrible darkness Christ came with the light of life. More than just his words and works, the very divine life from which they sprang beamed forth the light of a life that shone in stark contrast to the darkness of corrupted human life — religious and otherwise. His death and resurrection opened a door of hope that men could be set free from the dominion of sin and death and come to possess that life — God's life.

As the good news was proclaimed and thousands began to believe, Satan opposed what was happening with every means at his disposal. He hates Christ and any true follower of Christ can expect to be a special target. Christ's victory at the cross spells Satan's ultimate defeat — and he knows it. That victory was won on behalf of those from every nation and age who put their trust in Christ.

Satan's very nature is that of a liar and a deceiver. It is no surprise, therefore, that one of his chief weapons against Christ's true followers has been deception, in particular, religious deception. He comes offering a different Jesus, a different spirit, a different gospel. 2 Cor. 11:4. Of course he is careful to disguise these substitutes so that they appear to be the real thing.

In warning the Corinthians against false ministries Paul describes them as, "false apostles, deceitful workmen, masquerading as apostles of Christ. And no wonder, for Satan himself masquerades as an angel of light. It is not surprising, then, if his servants masquerade as servants of righteousness." 2 Cor. 11:13-15. The devil wouldn't accomplish much if he approached Christians as a "devil of darkness"! No! His aim is that men should receive him and his servants as heaven-sent.

Of course Satan has made — and continues to make — wide use of direct persecution against the followers of Jesus. However, this has often resulted in a stronger, healthier church that grows in spite of all his efforts to stamp it out. Deception has been by far his most effective weapon.

All-Out War

I believe it is safe to say that deception will reach its peak right before the coming of Christ. 2 Thess. 2:8 tells us of a "lawless one" who will be destroyed at Christ's coming. Verses 9-12 tell us, "The coming of the lawless one will be in accordance with the work of Satan displayed in all kinds of counterfeit miracles, signs and wonders, and in every sort of evil that deceives those who are perishing. They perish because they refused to love the truth and so be saved. For this reason God sends them a powerful delusion so that they will believe the lie and so that all will be condemned who have not believed the truth but have delighted in wickedness."

That is a picture of Satan mounting an all-out effort as he senses the end nearing. What a terrible hold he will have on all who have rejected truth in that hour. God Himself will send them a "powerful delusion." The remnant of true believers will need God as we've never needed Him before in order to stand in such an hour. What a wonderful promise we have in the words of Jesus: "...surely I am with you always, to the very end of the age." Matt. 28:20.

One area that needs to be explored concerns the deceiver. What is a deceiver like? How would you recognize one? Of course we need to quickly acknowledge the imperfections of God's true servants and recognize that God works through them in spite of those imperfections. Still, there is a difference between a divinely-anointed but imperfect man and a deceiver sent and anointed by Satan. And I believe the Lord can help us to distinguish between them.

Satan's Style of Leadership

When I think of the kind of religious leadership Satan promotes I think of Satan himself. Words like "dominion" and "control" come to mind. Isaiah 14:13-14 says of him, "You said in your heart, 'I will ascend to heaven; I will raise my throne above the stars of God; I will sit enthroned on the mount of assembly, on the utmost heights of the sacred mountain. I will ascend above the tops of the clouds; I will make myself like the Most High.'"

Satan may have set out to make himself like the Most High but he is not like Him at all. He is utterly selfish, focused only on his own ambitions, caring nothing for his subjects, wanting only to "sit enthroned." That is why the scriptures use such words as "murderer" (John 8:44) and "Apollyon," which means "destroyer," (Rev. 9:11) to describe him. He will give his subjects the illusion of freedom while keeping them firmly under his control.

His nature can readily be seen in the lives of those out of whom Jesus cast devils. Those devils had no interest whatsoever in bettering the lives of their victims, only in using, abusing, and ultimately destroying them and moving on to other victims. They were all about absolute control and it took divine authority to pry them loose and force them to leave.

We can see the kind of leadership Satan encourages in the words of Jesus in Luke 22:25-26, "The kings of the Gentiles lord it over them; and those who exercise authority over them call themselves Benefactors." In these words we can see not only the spirit of dominion but also a self-deception in that the rulers actually think of themselves as Benefactors! "I have total control over you and it's for your good!"

Listen to the words of Jesus as he draws a contrast: "But you are not to be like that. Instead, the greatest among you should be like the youngest, and the one who rules like the one who serves." Luke 22:26. And so we have *dominion leadership* on the one hand and *servant leadership* on the other. It is not a question of whether there is to be leadership but rather the *character* of that leadership.

Jesus himself is the greatest example of true spiritual leadership. He did not come as a king but as a humble servant. Phil. 2:7-8. In Mark 10:45 Jesus said, "For even the Son of Man did not come to be served, but to serve, and to give his life as a ransom for many." In John 13 we see Jesus giving a graphic demonstration of this principle by literally taking on the role of a servant, a slave, and washing his disciples' feet. "You call me 'Teacher' and 'Lord,' and rightly so, for that is what I am. Now that I, your Lord and Teacher, have washed your feet, you also should wash one another's feet. I have set you an example that you should do as I have done for you." Verses 13-15.

One Example

As I survey the religious landscape today I'm afraid that much of what I see in the way of spiritual leadership bears little resemblance to what Jesus taught. More than that, much of it smells more like dominion.

A few years back Bro. Jimmy Robbins and I were returning from an overseas trip. As we began our journey home we went into a little cafe in the airport for a cup of coffee and fell into conversation with a young lady working there. As we spoke it became evident that she loved the Lord and wanted to serve him.

It also became evident that she was enmeshed in a religious system that had her starved, spiritually stifled and terrified to question. She was buried under many layers of supposed spiritual "authority" as a result of a widely-advocated system of church growth and it was killing her spiritually. She was terrified that if she so much as questioned anything or anyone she would be in rebellion against God and He would judge her. And the one under whose direct authority she had been placed was, to say the least, no spiritual help.

One immediate issue concerned a job opportunity she was considering that would better provide for her family's many needs. But it had been drummed into her that apart from "permission" from the "chain of command" above her she would be in defiance of God's authority. She was trembling as she even spoke about it. It is one thing to seek wisdom and counsel, but "permission"?! That's precisely the kind of "leadership" Jesus warned his disciples against!

In the few minutes we had we both tried to encourage her that the kind of dominion authority she was describing was not of God. She didn't express any of this in a spirit of rebellion but seemed more like an abused sheep simply crying out for the freedom to serve God and grow spiritually. We encouraged her to honestly seek God to lead her and then committed her into the Lord's hands.

I confess to a good deal of anger when I see and hear of the Lord's sheep being abused and intimidated in religious systems like that. The Spirit of Christ is all about loving, serving, and nurturing the sheep, leading them to good pastures. But that's not what Satan promotes. He wants control, whether obvious in what I described above or subtle as is often the case.

Old and New Testament Leadership

One way Satan takes advantage of people in this area is to blur the differences between the Old and New Testaments. In the Old Testament we see God, in order to fulfill His purposes, establishing a relationship with the nation of Israel based on a covenant of laws. God is a holy God and most of the Israelites were unbelieving idolaters at heart — and the best of them were still sinners. Thus the relationship was necessarily an "arms-length" one.

God's presence dwelled in a very special place, the holy of holies, first in the tabernacle and later in the temple. There the ark of the covenant, the cherubim, and the mercy seat were located. Anyone going in there would instantly die. The only exception was the high priest who went in just once a year on the day of atonement. Even then he followed elaborate cleansing rituals and only went in with blood, as well as incense so that the smoke would obscure the mercy seat. Otherwise even he would die. See Leviticus 16.

All of this was meant to teach the people about God's holiness and their sinfulness and need. The people themselves did not have direct access to God. Special men were needed as intermediaries. If the people sinned and needed to offer a sacrifice they went to a priest and he offered it on their behalf. If they wanted to inquire of the Lord about something they went to a prophet or a priest and he delivered whatever word the Lord gave. In addition, as time went along, kings ruled with absolute authority.

These men were themselves set apart — sanctified — in special ways so they could serve in these roles. Priests went through their rituals of cleansing before they could carry out the duties of their office. When Isaiah the prophet was caught up to see the Lord's glory in chapter 6, he became deeply conscious of his own sinfulness — but the Lord Himself provided the needed cleansing and then commissioned him with a special ministry to Israel. David was anointed with oil to be king. Some men filled their roles in a godly manner while others did not.

It is all too common in our day for religious leaders to appeal to Old Testament prophets and priests in order to justify a dominion-style leadership — with them having the dominion, of course! How many men have quoted Psalm 105:15 (KJV) which says, "Touch not mine anointed, and do my prophets no harm," to prop up their position of authority over their followers?! What many of them mean, however, is, "How dare you question me?!"

However we must point out that even though men in the Old Testament were given authority over other men, the *character* of that leadership was never intended by God to be like that of the world. He intended prophet, priest, and king to use their authority in righteousness to serve the people.

We think of Moses as a powerful and eloquent man, commanding respect by sheer force of his personality. That is how Hollywood has portrayed him. In reality he was anything but! He is described in Num. 12:3 as "a very humble man, more humble than anyone else on the face of the earth." When God called him he tried everything he could think of to talk the Lord out of it, citing his inability even to speak. The Lord finally told him that Aaron, his brother, could be his spokesman. Yet Moses was the greatest of the Old Testament prophets by far, not because he was high and mighty in himself but because, in his weakness he received divine strength to serve the people. Even then his leadership was marked by a spirit of humility. He relied on God to fight his battles.

Under the new covenant everything changed. We have One alone Who is Prophet, Priest, and King, our Lord Jesus. Christ Himself has filled all of the mediatorial roles. Every believer has access to God freely through Him. Eph. 2:14-22. When he cried on the cross, "It is finished," the large curtain that hid the holy of holies was torn from top to bottom. Matt. 27:50-51; John 19:30. God Himself had opened the way into the holiest because of the blood of Jesus! Hebrews, chapter 9, and 10:19-22. When it comes to the priesthood, we are all priests. 1 Peter 2:5, 9, Rev. 1:6, 5:10.

They Will All Know Me

In Joel 2:28-29 we find this wonderful word of prophecy about what was to come: "I will pour out my Spirit on all people. Your sons and daughters will prophesy, your old men will dream dreams, your young men will see visions. Even on my servants, both men and women, I will pour out my Spirit in those days." No longer were such things restricted to a select few.

In Jer. 31:34 we find the prophecy quoted in Hebrew 8:11, "...they will all know me, from the least of them to the greatest." No longer were there to be special classes of men that stood between the people and their God. Everyone could approach Him freely. There is only one mediator and that is Jesus Christ himself. 1 Timothy 2:5.

In Matthew 23 Jesus strongly denounced the religious leadership of the Jews. In verses 8-12 he said, "But you are not to be called 'Rabbi,' for you have only one Master and you are all brothers. And do not call anyone on earth 'father,' for you have one Father, and he is in heaven. Nor are you to be called 'teacher,' for you have one Teacher, the Christ. The greatest among you will be your servant. For whoever exalts himself will be humbled, and whoever humbles himself will be exalted."

Note carefully the words, "...you have only one Master and you are all brothers." Surely that defines clearly the relationships that exist in God's kingdom. It is a simple picture. Even though gifts and callings among men may differ only One is in charge. Christ is the head of the church which is his body. Eph. 1:22-23. All the rest are brethren, varying in function, serving one another, but none having spiritual dominion over others. Whenever anyone, supposedly in Christ's name, lifts himself up and exercises *dominion* over others, Satan's hand is at work.

An Exhortation to Elders

Does that do away with human leadership? Of course not! It just defines its character. Consider what Peter wrote in 1 Peter, chapter 5. In verses 1-4 he writes, "To the elders among you, I appeal as a fellow elder, a witness of Christ's sufferings and one who also will share in the glory to be revealed: Be shepherds of God's flock that is under your care, serving as overseers — not because you must, but because you are willing, as God wants you to be; not greedy for money, but eager to serve; not lording it over those entrusted to you, but being examples to the flock. And when the Chief Shepherd appears, you will receive the crown of glory that will never fade away."

Note that Peter does not assume a high position *above* his readers. He does not talk "down" to them. Remember, this is Peter we're talking about, one of the original apostles. Yet he does not "command," but rather "appeals." And even this appeal is not made from "above" but as a "fellow elder." His gift and calling were indeed special but his language conveys a man standing *beside* and *among* his readers, not someone high and mighty and ruling over them. This fact sets the tone for the entire exhortation.

Peter begins with the simple words, "Be shepherds of God's flock that is under your care...." Words like "shepherds" and "care" surely remind of us of the description of our Lord Jesus as the "good shepherd" who "lays his life down for the sheep." John 10:11. Remember also the wonderful prophecy of Isaiah 40:11: "He tends his flock like a shepherd: He gathers the lambs in his arms and carries them close to his heart; he gently leads those that have young." There is nothing selfish or abusive in a good shepherd. Rather his personal interests are set aside and his efforts are directed to the welfare of the sheep. He is a servant.

Peter refers to the flock as "God's flock," reminding his readers Whose the sheep are. The shepherd is a servant, not only to the sheep, but also to the God to Whom they belong. The sheep do not "belong" to the shepherd nor are they there to serve the interests of the shepherd; it is the other way around. The shepherd is not the center of things; the sheep are. It is not his will that is to prevail; it is that of the "Chief Shepherd," our Lord Jesus Christ, the only Head of the church.

It is in the light of these simple truths that Peter highlights three particular areas of concern when it comes to "shepherding." The first area concerns the willingness to do it. Peter says in verse 2, "...not because you must, but because you are willing, as God wants you to be...." We are selfish creatures by nature and the interests of self must be laid aside in order to properly serve the sheep. This selfish nature causes some to be grudging, to act out of mere duty, even to be resentful of the demands of shepherding. God wants shepherds who serve with a willing heart, following the example of our Lord himself. His spirit of willingness took him all the way to the cross — even with joy! Heb. 12:2.

The second issue Peter tackled was this: "...not greedy for money, but eager to serve...." Should not these simple words cause us to cringe as we survey the religious landscape of today? In this instance the so-called shepherd, instead of grudgingly withholding service, uses the guise of service to serve his own selfish financial interests. The sheep, the work, become a means to a very selfish end. Such a man does not serve Christ at all and it is the sheep who suffer.

Not Lords

The third issue is the particular one that Christ highlighted: (verse 3) "...not lording it over those entrusted to you, but being examples to the flock." In verse 2 Peter had referred to elders as "overseers" yet he now adds, "not lording it over those entrusted to you." It is difficult for human beings to understand how those two ideas can function together. We are prone to think of an "overseer" as one "in charge," a boss, one possessing authority and commanding obedience from those beneath him. Yet God desires overseers who are not "overlords." There is a monumental difference. The overseer is to lead by example. The overlord leads through control. It is only by God's grace that it is possible to be a true shepherd.

Does that mean that there is no submission involved, that each one is to be a law unto himself? Of course not! In verse 5 Peter continues, "Young men, in the same way be submissive to those who are older." Two things are very significant in this verse. The younger ones are indeed told to be submissive. But the submission is not a blind obedience imposed from above. It is something to be willingly offered.

This is clear in that Peter also includes the words, "in the same way." In the same way as what? In the same way as the elders are encouraged to serve! Peter is saying that shepherding is itself a form of submission, a setting aside of the interests of self for the sake of the sheep. It, as we have noted, is to be a willing thing, a choice on the part of the shepherd to be a proper under-shepherd, that is, a servant.

Christ's Example

Think of the ministry of Christ. Did he go around demanding obedience from any and everyone? Of course not! He understood that among the people as a whole there were some who were God's sheep. Most were not. The sheep were the only ones capable of truly hearing his voice and because they were sheep they would *willingly* follow him. John 10:27-29. He did not need any kind of force, intimidation or psychology to obtain followers. Nor did he need to "control" them. His trust was in his Father Who worked with hearts.

In John 6 when multitudes stopped following him Jesus simply turned to the disciples and said, "Will ye also go away?" (John 6:67, KJV). Peter answered, "Lord, to whom shall we go? You have the words of eternal life. We believe and know that you are the Holy One of God." Verses 68-69. How is it that they knew who he was and others didn't? Very simply: it was revealed to them by God (see Matt. 16:17). Jesus didn't have to strive to convince them. They were so convinced they wouldn't leave! They weren't convinced because Jesus had somehow "brain-washed" them; he simply gave out the truth and his sheep were enabled to recognize that truth and to willingly follow.

When true shepherds lead true sheep there will be a willing heart on the part of the sheep not because submission is demanded but because they recognize the voice of the Divine Shepherd as He anoints those with leadership gifts. I don't mean to oversimplify or to gloss over problems that arise but what I have described is what God is after.

Leadership that demands obedience is modeled after Satan and not after Christ.

All of You

Lest the point be overlooked Peter continues, "All of you, clothe yourselves with humility toward one another, because, 'God opposes the proud but gives grace to the humble.'" (Verse 5). "All of you" certainly includes the elders and highlights the true character of relationships in the body of Christ. There are indeed leaders that God raises up yet everyone in the body is servant to everyone else and Christ alone is Head.

1 Peter 4:10-11 says, "Each one should use whatever gift he has received to serve others, faithfully administering God's grace in its various forms. If anyone speaks, he should do it as one speaking the very words of God. If anyone serves, he should do it with the strength God provides, so that in all things God may be praised through Jesus Christ. To him be the glory and the power for ever and ever. Amen." Peter's words include *everyone* in the body of Christ.

Wherever a body of believers truly walks in this order Satan cannot get in. Everyone gets their spiritual ability from Christ and uses that ability for the welfare of the whole. No one walks in self-will, pride and independence. Each one's will is gladly set aside and the will of God sought. Christ is honored as Head in a practical way and not just vaguely acknowledged as a sort of figurehead. I realize that I am describing the ideal but is this not what the church is supposed to be, what we are all supposed to be seeking? Is that not what the church was for a time after Pentecost?

It is no wonder that in his attempts to corrupt the church and lead it astray Satan has attacked this order in every way he can think of. Basically he has sought to disconnect the church from its Head and to raise up men to rule over other men. Of course, he seeks to raise up men who are actually under his influence and control, whether they are aware of it or not. He thereby becomes the head for all practical purposes. This is simply a manifestation of his fundamental desire to enthrone himself.

Chapter 2

Symptoms

We see Satan's influence everywhere in human society as men rule over other men. I understand that in a broken world God ordains rulers to restrain evil, however, such rule, though necessary, rarely reflects His character. That is why Jesus told his disciples not to be like them! Satan's own spirit of self-centered pride is expressed again and again as men pursue power and control in the name of leadership. (Isaiah 14:12-15). This principle has deeply corrupted Christianity, elevating men to positions of spiritual dominion over others that God never intended.

We have seen Peter, writing to elders not as a high and mighty apostle issuing commands to his lowly subjects, but as a fellow elder, encouraging them to lead by example, promoting a mutual humility and submission among all the believers — including the elders.

What a contrast his words are to the situation John described in 3 John 9-10, where he says, "I wrote to the church, but Diotrephes, who loves to be first, will have nothing to do with us. So if I come, I will call attention to what he is doing, gossiping maliciously about us. Not satisfied with that, he refuses to welcome the brothers. He also stops those who want to do so and puts them out of the church." Can you imagine someone so blind, so power-hungry, that he would refuse to recognize one of the original apostles chosen by Christ Himself! Sadly, the spirit of Diotrephes is very much alive and well in our day.

Listen to the Lord's indictment of the corrupt spiritual leadership in Israel at the time of Ezekiel: Ezek. 34:2-4 says, "Woe to the shepherds of Israel who only take care of themselves! Should not shepherds take care of the flock? You eat the curds, clothe yourselves with the wool and slaughter the choice animals, but you do not take care of the flock. You have not strengthened the weak or healed the sick or bound up the injured. You have not brought back the strays or searched for the lost. You have ruled them harshly and brutally." What a picture of self-centered dominion leadership! Surely it is obvious that the inspiration behind such leadership bears the mark of the serpent. Yet, do not we see these same characteristics in many places today?

Ruling Classes

Given the corrupted nature of men it is inevitable that whenever men are elevated above others such abuses will occur. Satan has badly corrupted the church over the centuries by promoting an order that divides God's people into different classes. God intended all believers to serve one another in love using their various divinely given abilities. Satan has sought to turn many of these gifts and callings into ruling classes.

And so we see religious systems with popes, bishops, priests, apostles, prophets, pastors, and many other titles thought to denote *offices* with dominion authority over others. We have been taught to accept such class distinctions as clergy and laity, ministry and people, etc., as normal Christianity, the way it is supposed to be.

For example, there has been a lot of emphasis in some circles on the so-called "five-fold ministry." This is taken from Ephesians 4:11 where Christ is referred to as having given "some to be apostles, some to be prophets, some to be evangelists, and some to be pastors and teachers." Indeed He did give such gifts to the church and we see them function throughout the New Testament as servants to the church, respected and honored, but as servants.

These special gifts were given for the purpose of equipping the saints that they, the saints, might do the work of ministering. They were never intended to establish a special class lifted far above the common believer, elevated to a special high place between the people and God and commanding unquestioning obedience.

Titles

Often, a symptom of Satan's influence can be seen in an emphasis upon honorific titles conferred upon those who occupy these special "high offices." Jesus made note of this characteristic of the religious leadership in his day. As quoted earlier he said of them: "…they love the place of honor at banquets and the most important seats in the synagogues;

they love to be greeted in the marketplaces and to have men call them 'Rabbi.' But you are not to be called 'Rabbi,' for you have only one Master and you are all brothers. And do not call anyone on earth 'father,' for you have one Father, and he is in heaven. Nor are you to be called 'teacher,' for you have one Teacher, the Christ. The greatest among you will be your servant. For whoever exalts himself will be humbled, and whoever humbles himself will be exalted." Matt. 23:6-12.

But how many in our day are content to be just "brother" or "servant"? Instead they love to be called, "Reverend," "The Very Right Reverend," "Bishop," "Doctor," "Apostle," "Prophet," etc. This sort of thing is nothing but pride and self-exaltation in direct defiance of the plain words of Jesus. It certainly does not reflect the spirit of Jesus or that of the first apostles. The word "apostle" simply means "sent one" and designates their gift and calling, not some high ecclesiastical title by which they lorded it over others.

I remember hearing a man speak awhile back who was widely known as "Dr. So-and-So." In actual fact his "doctorate" had been conferred upon him by a very doubtful source. In spite of this the man was so attached to his title that it had virtually become a part of his name. Anyone who forgot would be quickly reminded about the "Doctor" part. The man — who claimed to be a Christian and have a ministry — was eaten up with pride and it colored everything he did.

In contrast there are many men and women who have earned legitimate doctorates yet who do not use their titles in pride to lift themselves up above others. And no doubt there are those who have been tagged with titles like "Reverend" who are not proud. Nevertheless I am persuaded that most religious "titles" in our day are worthless and reflect the apostasy of the church.

"Prophets"

This seems especially true of the many who insist upon being called, "Apostle," or "Prophet." Paul contended with such men in his day. Of some he wrote: "For such men are false apostles, deceitful workmen, masquerading as apostles of Christ. And no wonder, for Satan himself masquerades as an angel of light. It is not surprising, then, if his servants masquerade as servants of righteousness. Their end will be what their actions deserve." 2 Cor. 11:13-15.

I confess to being sick and tired of the many grandiose pronouncements that come across my desk from time to time from such self-appointed prophets. They vainly imagine themselves to be in the mold of Old Testament prophets like Elijah or Jeremiah, wielding authority over cities and nations, privy to great spiritual secrets and insights hidden from lesser people. Their followers "ooh" and "aah" over the latest supposed "revelations" and glory in their access to such high "prophetic" spiritual realms.

I've seen so many of these so-called "prophecies" that seem to have no connection whatever with reality. Each new revelation is gloried over and just as quickly forgotten as newer "revelations" come. Can God speak today? Certainly, He can, but most of what I've encountered is nothing but fantasy and delusion.

I wonder how many such prophets, who would like to be thought of as being like Elijah, would like to be judged by the Old Testament standard set forth in Deut. 18:20-22? "But a prophet who presumes to speak in my name anything I have not commanded him to say, or a prophet who speaks in the name of other gods, must be put to death. You may say to yourselves, 'How can we know when a message has not been spoken by the Lord?' If what a prophet proclaims in the name of the Lord does not take place or come true, that is a message the Lord has not spoken. That prophet has spoken presumptuously. Do not be afraid of him.'"

We have pointed out that many believers have been intimidated into fearful silence, afraid even to ask an honest question, through the misuse of Psalm 105:15 where we read, "Do not touch my anointed ones; do my prophets no harm." Where spiritual leaders truly are sent and anointed by God there is no need to intimidate the sheep into submission. They do not need to be subjugated and controlled. God's sheep recognize the Lord's voice expressed by the anointing and willingly follow. A spirit of intimidation should be a major "red flag." Something is very wrong.

This perversion of God's intent with respect to spiritual leadership is deception and plays a large role in Satan's corruption of the church. It is surely right to note that there are many good and sincere servants of the Lord who seek to minister within this system, thinking it is scriptural, but the fact is that it opens the door to a whole host of opportunities for Satan to work.

He causes the most damage where he is able to place one of his servants, someone he controls, into a position of leadership. Through such leaders Satan himself becomes the effective leader and people are led astray. Instead of people being brought into the freedom Christ purchased with His blood, they are shut up in spiritual prisons, controlled through fear and many forms of deception.

Before it is over I believe the Lord is going to destroy these prisons and bring His people out.

Men Exalted

Satan lifted himself up — and so do many of his servants. Where there is an undue emphasis on human personalities then Satan's hand is at work. We see men lifted up as "God's great man of the hour," or some similar expression that exalts the man or men involved. Sometimes the man himself will create and encourage this emphasis and other times those around him will do it, sometimes both. The end result is that the real focus is more upon the man than it is upon Christ. Sometimes this is done subtly and other times very openly.

Many of the great religious works of our day revolve entirely around some personality who is greatly exalted and blindly followed. People gravitate to such leaders in an attempt to silence their own uncertainty and confusion. It is as though these personalities stand between the people and God, dispensing His words and blessings. But don't dare to question!

Consider some of the great religious personalities of our day in the light of Paul's simple words in 2 Cor. 4:5 — "For we do not preach ourselves, but Jesus Christ as Lord, and ourselves as your servants for Jesus' sake." "*We do not preach ourselves....*" Christ was the center of Paul's message. Paul saw himself as just a servant — a slave. He saw Christ as the only one worthy of being the center of attention. God's great man of the hour — of every hour — is Christ and Christ alone. Something is not right when human personalities usurp His rightful place.

When religious leaders are constantly drawing attention to themselves, lifting themselves up, when those around him encourage this exaltation and intimidate questioners — run! The Spirit that anoints God's true servants will point men to Christ. The Spirit of Christ will never cause men to seek the spotlight for themselves. He alone is our message, the center and focus of everything.

The spirit of self-exaltation is simply a path to control. The serpent is behind it.

Pride is very much at the heart of such a spirit. Religion is full of pride. Religious leaders readily bask in the praise of men and gullible followers just as readily heap it on them.

Think about Paul. He really *did* occupy a special place in God's plan, a plan that included great revelations such as being caught up to the "third heaven." There he heard things he couldn't even talk about. Paul was made of the same stuff as the rest of us. How many men could experience such things and remain free from pride? Approximately none!

Paul's Special Gift

God, of course, understood this perfectly and so He arranged a special gift for Paul to help him deal with this weakness. This special "gift" was a demon that harassed Paul and made his life difficult. Read his account of this in 2 Corinthians 12. Paul did what any of us would do: he prayed — earnestly! Finally God revealed to Paul the purpose of this "thorn" and his attitude changed completely. He came to understand that the thorn was given to "keep him from becoming conceited."

He even learned to glory in his weakness, seeing this not as a hindrance to ministry but rather as a path to God's power being manifested through him and his ministry being effective. He discovered in experience the truth of God's answer, "My grace is sufficient for you, for my power is made perfect in weakness." 2 Cor. 12:9. How many of today's spiritual leaders are even honest about, let alone glory in their weakness?

When you find someone of spiritual influence going on and on in uncorrected pride, something is wrong! Pride is not a product of God's Spirit. It comes from Lucifer by way of our fallen nature. Everyone contends with it but God disciplines His own. Those who are not disciplined by God are simply not His sons. Hebrews 12:8. Now, don't go around with a magnifying glass looking for faults in God's servants. You will surely find them! But God deals with His own.

Self Will

Another characteristic that often accompanies deception is a spirit of self-will. When a religious leader refuses to listen to anyone else but rather imposes his will on everyone around him, something is very wrong. That too is a tactic of control and is rooted in fallen human nature and not in the Spirit of Christ. Of course this characteristic could also apply to more than one who exercise control together.

We see this in John's description of the spirit of antichrist in 1 John 4. He speaks of false prophets who would come among the people, yet refuse to recognize the Christ that resided in His body. They would be the sort that acted as though they had a private "pipeline" to God. People were supposed to listen to them but they themselves were subject to no one but themselves.

John sums it up in 1 John 4:5-6 — "They are from the world and therefore speak from the viewpoint of the world, and the world listens to them. We are from God, and whoever knows God listens to us; but whoever is not from God does not listen to us. This is how we recognize the Spirit of truth and the spirit of falsehood."

Part of Peter's description of false prophets includes these words in 2 Peter 2:10 — "...them that walk after the flesh in the lust of uncleanness, and despise government. Presumptuous are they, selfwilled, they are not afraid to speak evil of dignities." KJV. Jude uses similar language in Jude 8 where he says, "… these dreamers pollute their own bodies, reject authority and slander celestial beings."

There is no higher earthly authority in spiritual matters than the church. Matthew 18:15-18. The church is not one man. It is a many-membered body. Remember again that Peter taught that everyone — elders included — were to be subject one to another in a spirit of humility. I Peter 5:5.

The true servant of Christ honors him and seeks His will, not his own. The self-willed man will intimidate, manipulate, flatter, bribe, and — in short — do whatever it takes to get his own way.

Love of Money

Another warning sign would come under the heading of self-gratification on the part of leaders. This would include those who bask in the praise of men as we mentioned above but a major part of self-gratification includes a love of material prosperity. The religious landscape of our day is littered with ministers who enjoy a luxurious lifestyle far beyond that of those they supposedly serve.

The scriptures are so clear about this sort of thing it is a wonder people fall for it. We quoted the words of Ezekiel in 34:2-3: "Woe to the shepherds of Israel who only take care of themselves! Should not shepherds take care of the flock? You eat the curds, clothe yourselves with the wool and slaughter the choice animals, but you do not take care of the flock." See also verse 8 where the Lord says, "… my shepherds did not search for my flock but cared for themselves rather than for my flock."

Remember also 1 Peter 5:2 where elders are instructed not to be "greedy for money, but eager to serve." How different are so many today from Jesus and the apostles! To one who would follow him Jesus said in Matt. 8:20, "Foxes have holes and birds of the air have nests, but the Son of Man has no place to lay his head." To the rich young ruler Jesus said, "Sell everything you have and give to the poor, and you will have treasure in heaven. Then come, follow me." Luke 18:22. That was enough to turn this man aside. He valued his earthly riches above eternal life.

To all Jesus said, "If anyone would come after me, he must deny himself and take up his cross daily and follow me." Luke 9:23. There is no way an honest reading of the scriptures can result in the idea that following Jesus is a path to earthly self-gratification in any form. As Jesus simply said in Matt. 6:24, "You cannot serve both God and Money."

Part of the spirit of deception in this area is that material prosperity has been turned into a spiritual virtue, a sign of divine favor. How do you know God looks on you with favor? He blesses you with good health and financial success. That's the message. The preacher, himself a servant of money, preaches a so-called "prosperity gospel"; his gullible followers lavish material benefits upon him; and he flaunts it as a sign of divine favor, proof that his message is true. Paul wrote to Timothy about "men of corrupt mind, who have been robbed of the truth and who think that godliness is a means to financial gain." 1 Tim. 6:5.

Listen to Paul's following words: "But godliness with contentment is great gain. For we brought nothing into the world, and we can take nothing out of it. But if we have food and clothing, we will be content with that. People who want to get rich fall into temptation and a trap and into many foolish and harmful desires that plunge men into ruin and destruction. For the love of money is a root of all kinds of evil. Some people, eager for money, have wandered from the faith and pierced themselves with many griefs. But you, man of God, flee from all this...." 1 Tim. 6:6-11.

Very often you will see preachers infected with the love of money telling the people, "Give to me (or my ministry) and God will prosper you." What a horrible twisting of the spirit and intent of the scriptures! Can you imagine Jesus or Paul or Peter raising money that way? Giving is treated as a financial investment. A pitch like that appeals to the desires of religious unbelievers whose motive is transparent: they seek earthly prosperity.

Even worse is when poor and needy people are persuaded to give sacrificially in hopes of bettering themselves materially — while the religious leader lives in luxury. I would hate to be such a leader on the Day of Judgment. Jesus, in contrast, told people of a heavenly Father who knew of their earthly needs and that they were not to seek those things. Rather they were to seek "first his kingdom and his righteousness, and all these things will be given to you as well." Matt. 6:33.

God is not stupid! He is not fooled for a moment by those who attempt to dress up greed in religious clothes and pass it off as something spiritual. Money is not evil in itself; it is the love of it that opens the door for Satan to corrupt everything we touch.

Hypocrisy

Another obvious area of self-gratification has to do with immorality in its various forms. How many there are today who could be described by Peter's words: "For they mouth empty, boastful words and, by appealing to the lustful desires of sinful human nature, they entice people who are just escaping from those who live in error. They promise them freedom, while they themselves are slaves of depravity — for a man is a slave to whatever has mastered him." 2 Peter 2:18-19.

Religion in our day is full of hypocrisy — and Satan loves it. He rejoices at every moral scandal from some supposed servant of Christ. A true servant of Christ has a real battle — as does every believer — with his old nature, learning to subdue it through God's strength and provision. But that is a far cry from the many who simply live a double life, dominated by fleshly desires: the prominent minister who tells a dirty joke and moments later steps into the pulpit and acts real spiritual, seemingly with no conscience; the evangelist who preaches the great sermon and then sneaks off to engage in some sort of sexual immorality.

Several years ago a brother and I were traveling overseas, visiting Christian believers in various villages. Our driver was a hired professional and had been born into another religion. In the course of his work he had often driven ministers around and he commented to us how many of them were one thing before the people and another altogether when they got back into the car. He rightly recognized their hypocrisy. I'm thankful to say that he testified to seeing something different in us, to God's glory alone. He was also around a true ministry in his own country and has since come to Christ!

One thing that helps to produce this kind of hypocrisy is an emphasis upon power, manifestation, and miracles, rather than on godly character. It should be very obvious from the Word that such an emphasis is wrong — and dangerous. Satan is very much in the sign and wonder business. Anyone who bases their discernment on signs and wonders is asking to be deceived.

Paul's ministry was attended by many supernatural miracles yet see what he says in 1 Corinthians 9. He speaks of his ministry and compares it to running a race, seeking a prize. Of course the prize he sought was eternal and not like the short-lived prize won in an earthly footrace. And so in 1 Cor. 9:26-27 he says, "Therefore I do not run like a man running aimlessly; I do not fight like a man beating the air. No, I beat my body and make it my slave so that after I have preached to others, I myself will not be disqualified for the prize." The thing that would disqualify him from usefulness to the Lord would be to be ruled by his fleshly appetites.

To Timothy he wrote: "In a large house there are articles not only of gold and silver, but also of wood and clay; some are for noble purposes and some for ignoble. If a man cleanses himself from the latter, he will be an instrument for noble purposes, made holy, useful to the Master and prepared to do any good work. Flee the evil desires of youth, and pursue righteousness, faith, love and peace, along with those who call on the Lord out of a pure heart." 2 Tim. 2:20-23.

Where power and manifestation are valued above godliness something is wrong.

As we said earlier, we have set out, not to produce a complete catalog of deception, but rather some characteristics. Thus far we have focused mostly on deceivers, agents of deception and warning signs that something is not right. It would be well at this point to summarize what we have said simply as...

Some Head Other Than Christ

When you think of it that is the essence of the matter. The true church has only one Head. That Head is Christ. He was never meant to be a mere figurehead while men actually ran things. Wherever the Headship of Christ is abandoned or compromised in some way, deception and spiritual apostasy follows. It may proceed gradually, but it does proceed. The more men exercise control, the more influence Satan has until he has fully usurped the place that rightly belongs to Christ alone. God put His Son in charge. The government is on His shoulders (Isaiah 6:6-7). He — and He alone — is the Head of His Body, the Church. Colossians 1:18.

Nevertheless the ultimate deceiver, Satan, has widely succeeded in undermining God's order by promoting the rule of men. He doesn't mind too much when Christ is verbally acknowledged as Head as long as men actually run things. In far too many places Jesus truly is a mere figurehead with little or no influence on what goes on.

The leadership of men inevitably reflects their fallen sinful condition, characterized by such things as pride and the desire to be "in control." Satan has little trouble tightening his grip whenever men try to operate apart from the true Headship of Christ. It is a road that leads downhill into spiritual darkness.

The discerning reader will recognize that this issue affects much of the religious world, both denominational and non-denominational. Some, recognizing the tendency of denominations to become tradition-bound institutions ruled by men, have "come out," but to what? Too often the "non-denominational" result is no better. Is Christ really the active Head or isn't He? That is the real issue. Whenever men actually run things, deception has taken root.

The particulars we have mentioned are simply characteristics of the leadership and rule of men who operate apart from the Headship of Christ and consequently turn the faith once delivered to the saints into mere religion. Disconnecting the Body of Christ from her Head is obviously a critical part of Satan's efforts to deceive. If he can accomplish that everything else is easy. He has nothing to fear, even from dead orthodoxy. Good doctrine alone is not enough. We need the living presence and rule of Christ in our midst. Nothing less will do. We are no match for the devil. God's plan is simple: Christ in us, the hope of glory. Colossians 1:27.

Chapter 3

The Message

Another major area of Satan's attack concerns the message that is proclaimed. What is it that is preached and believed? Is it "the faith that was once for all entrusted to the saints" (Jude 3) or something else? Just because something is labeled "Christian" and the Bible is quoted doesn't necessarily mean it is "the faith" to which Jude referred. Satan loves to promote his lies under the banner of biblical truth. The truth, however, is all but buried in many places in our day under an avalanche of religious lies.

What is biblical truth? What is the standard? Well, what did Paul preach? Surely he had a clear grasp of the true gospel message. After all, God inspired him to write about half of the New Testament, giving him deep insight into His truth and purposes. The insight that Paul had was not the result of mere study and intellectual pursuit but rather was the result of divine revelation.

In Gal. 1:11-12 he wrote, "I want you to know, brothers, that the gospel I preached is not something that man made up. I did not receive it from any man, nor was I taught it; rather, I received it by revelation from Jesus Christ." Paul had a special divine call to proclaim God's message in a pagan world. Not only that, he often had to defend that message against false teachers.

And Paul wasn't exactly shy in his defense of the truth. In Gal. 1:6-8 he wrote, "I am astonished that you are so quickly deserting the one who called you by the grace of Christ and are turning to a different gospel — which is really no gospel at all. Evidently some people are throwing you into confusion and are trying to pervert the gospel of Christ. But even if we or an angel from heaven should preach a gospel other than the one we preached to you, let him be eternally condemned!" Paul actually wished that God would cast these false teachers into hell!

What conviction! What certainty! The watchword of our day is, "Whatever...." I believe this; you believe that: "Whatever." None of that for Paul! He understood what was at stake. He knew that there was such a thing as real objective truth. He knew that there was but one message by which men could be saved. He daily laid his life on the line to proclaim the only hope available to his hearers.

He didn't dare to give out any other message when men's eternal destinies were hanging in the balance. And he therefore had no tolerance for what he knew to be false gospels that led people to believe they were headed for heaven when they were actually on the road to the lake of fire. May God give us today the same clarity, not in defense of our cherished traditions, but in devotion to His Word and His purpose as He reveals them.

Paul's Message

So what did Paul preach? When he came to a city, either to preach to the lost or to build up a church, what was his message? We do not have to guess. In 1 Cor. 2:1-2 he wrote, "When I came to you, brothers, I did not come with eloquence or superior wisdom as I proclaimed to you the testimony about God. For I resolved to know nothing while I was with you except Jesus Christ and him crucified."

Nothing! No other message. "Jesus Christ and him crucified." That's it! Two things: the person of Jesus Christ, the Son of God — who He is; and what He accomplished when He was crucified. Grasp that message and you stand on solid ground. Miss it and you miss everything.

But how can that be? Didn't Paul preach on other subjects like marriage, Christian living, church order, Christ's coming, giving, etc.? Yes, of course he did, but Paul understood the essential message in a way that I believe few understand in our day. He understood that there was only one foundation and that every other aspect of truth rises from that foundation and is vitally connected with it. Every aspect of biblical truth literally flows from and is utterly dependent on who Christ is and what He accomplished. Disconnect anything in the Bible from that foundation and the end result is manmade religion that can't help anyone.

Far too often the truth of "Jesus Christ and him crucified" has been reduced to a trite religious formula that people rush by to get to what they really want. They have no real understanding of the message. They get "saved" without ever truly knowing, as a result of Holy Spirit conviction, what it is to be lost. They join churches and profess to be followers of Jesus despite manifestly unchanged hearts. They seek happiness, fulfillment, meaning, fellowship, healing, signs and wonders, success, recognition and praise from men, etc. These self-centered goals play a large part in where they "go to church" while they miss what Paul was talking about completely. Paul understood that...

God Has a Purpose

It may sound strange to some but the gospel message is focused on God's purpose and NOT on man's needs and desires. That doesn't mean that He is uncaring or unconcerned about our needs. Not at all. It just means that we need to see everything in the light of His revealed purpose and not what we think we need and want. He created us in His image (Genesis 1:27). He must have had a reason. He must have had something particular in mind in so endowing us.

We see a glimpse of His purpose in the creation itself, a world of beauty and harmony in which Adam and his wife Eve enjoyed a close relationship with Him and had no unmet needs. There was no evil, no suffering, no pain, no death, only joy and fulfillment. God wonderfully revealed his loving nature, His character. Anyone who blames God for the mess this world is in simply doesn't understand.

Of course love is not meant to be a one-way relationship in which one gives and the other only takes. Love is meant to be mutual. God's love is only fulfilled when that love is reproduced in those He loves.

In Matt. 22:36 we find one of the religious leaders, a Pharisee, testing Jesus with a question. That question was, "Teacher, which is the greatest commandment in the Law?" Of course, the real motivation behind the question was not to learn truth but rather to discredit Jesus.

Nevertheless Jesus replies in verses 37-40, "'Love the Lord your God with all your heart and with all your soul and with all your mind.' This is the first and greatest commandment. And the second is like it: 'Love your neighbor as yourself.' All the Law and the Prophets hang on these two commandments." Jesus was quoting from Deut. 6:5-6 and Lev. 19:18.

At its essence the law of Moses was not just a bunch of "rules to live by." Rather, it was meant to point men towards a deep loving relationship with the eternal God and with each other. That's what He was after. It is His nature to love. We were made in His image and so love is what we were made for.

This is what we see at the end. For example, in Rev. 21:3-4 there is loud voice from the throne that says, "Now the dwelling of God is with men, and he will live with them. They will be his people, and God himself will be with them and be their God. He will wipe every tear from their eyes. There will be no more death or mourning or crying or pain, for the old order of things has passed away." God will finally have a people freed from everything that is evil, a people He can live with and love, a people set free to love as He does. Paradise restored.

Unfortunately Adam and Eve fell for the serpent's lies and embraced a different purpose: the pursuit of self-gratification. That purpose has dominated mankind ever since and is responsible for all that is evil in our world. All of our natural desires flow from that self-centered purpose, including religious ones.

Perversion of Nature

There is nothing worse than one created in the image of God devoted to living for self. It is a perversion of the very nature of things. We were not made for that purpose. Nothing but evil and death can result. What we call human nature is a cancer in God's universe, a cancer He will ultimately destroy. He can do no other and be Who He is.

He is light with no darkness at all. 1 John 1:5. Left to ourselves we are darkness with no light at all. Col. 1:13, 1 Peter 2:9, John 12:46. Our need is far more radical than many suppose. Sin has left us "broken" and unable to fix ourselves — even if we actually wanted to. As Paul points out in Rom. 3:11, "… there is no one who understands, no one who seeks God." And the worst thing is when men are exposed to light and *choose* darkness. John 3:19-20.

The true nature of God's love is revealed in John's simple words in 1 John 3:16: "This is how we know what love is: Jesus Christ laid down his life for us. And we ought to lay down our lives for our brothers." And Paul says in Rom 5:8, "But

God demonstrates his own love for us in this: While we were still sinners, Christ died for us."

God's love is focused on the object of His love to the point of self-sacrifice. It is not based upon any merit on the part of the one loved but upon the nature and purpose of the One who loves. What we humans call love falls far short of God's love. Yet, when He is through He will have a people who are as capable of loving Him as He is of loving them and all will be right again. Nothing short of a miracle can make that happen.

That is what the gospel — the good news — is about. It is about a God of unfathomable love reaching out to undeserving sinners to supernaturally rescue a people from sin and death and restore them to a place where they can fulfill His original purpose. Yet here we are hopelessly infected with purposes that are diametrically opposed to God's purpose. By nature we want the opposite of what He wants. Something has to change. Radically. God's answer is...

Nothing but Jesus

But what does that mean? It sounds nice but seems rather vague. Earlier we quoted from Paul's words in 2 Cor. 4:4-6, "The god of this age has blinded the minds of unbelievers, so that they cannot see the light of the gospel of the glory of Christ, who is the image of God. For we do not preach ourselves, but Jesus Christ as Lord, and ourselves as your servants for Jesus' sake. For God, who said, 'Let light shine out of darkness,' made his light shine in our hearts to give us the light of the knowledge of the glory of God in the face of Christ."

There is a lot in those verses. In verse 6 we see the God of creation Who simply spoke and light shone in darkness. He repeats that miracle every time He shines light into a sin-darkened heart. Notice that *He* is the One Who causes that to happen. Never forget that if it were not for His reaching out to us we would never seek or desire Him. That is how radically lost we are without Him.

What is that light? It is the knowledge of the glory of God. It is a revelation of God Himself, His nature and character. It is a revelation of His holiness, His love, His power, His purpose, and every other wonderful thing about Him. These are things we could never know apart from Him. They reveal in a measure what we turned away from in the beginning. And we all follow Adam's example. Romans 5:12.

But God is a spirit, unseen and invisible to mortal men. How can we truly know anything about such a One Who is so far removed from us? See how Paul describes Him in 1 Tim. 6:15-16, "God, the blessed and only Ruler, the King of kings and Lord of lords, who alone is immortal and who lives in unapproachable light, whom no one has seen or can see. To him be honor and might forever. Amen." He sounds pretty remote and impossible to reach even if we were inclined to seek Him, which we are not.

But according to Paul, this invisible God has an image! That image is Christ. If you want to know what God is like, look at Christ. Col. 1:15 tells us that "He is the image of the invisible God." Heb. 1:3 says, "The Son is the radiance of

God's glory and the exact representation of his being...." That is why a true revealed knowledge of Christ is so important. Without it we will have a distorted and false understanding of God Himself.

The Essential Truth About Jesus

Notice what it was that was the center of what Paul preached about Jesus according to 2 Cor. 4:5. His message was a seemingly simple one. He preached, "Jesus Christ as Lord." But what does that mean? To Paul, it meant everything. "Jesus Christ as Lord" is an all-encompassing truth with far-reaching implications for every human being and for the very world itself.

To begin with it was a revelation of who Jesus Christ was that transformed Paul's life when he was a zealous Pharisee named Saul. To Saul, Jesus had been an imposter, a false prophet who deserved to die. His followers needed to be crushed and their false religion stamped out. In his religious zeal he devoted himself to the task of arresting and killing followers of Jesus in the belief that in so doing he was faithfully serving God. What a picture of spiritual blindness! No one was better qualified than Paul was on that subject!

Then he met Jesus. The risen, glorious, divine Son of God appeared to him as he traveled to the city of Damascus to continue his persecution of Jesus' followers. In a short time he became one of those followers, all because of who Jesus was. The realization of this became the defining principle of Paul's life and ministry from that day on.

Jesus Christ is Lord! This was not a mere belief to be debated in the marketplace of religious ideas. It was a fact, an absolute truth to be proclaimed without compromise. It was a truth worth living and — if necessary — dying for. Men's destinies were determined by where they stood concerning Jesus Christ, the Son of God.

The Day of Pentecost

This was Peter's message on the day of Pentecost. He stood before a crowd of people guilty of the recent crucifixion of Christ and said, "… you, with the help of wicked men, put him to death by nailing him to the cross." Acts 2:23. What uncompromising boldness from a man who had so recently cowered in fear before a maid the night before that crucifixion. But things were different now. He and the others had met and spent time with the risen Savior, seen Him ascend into heaven, and had received the promised outpouring of the Spirit's power.

Filled with that power he boldly told them whom they had crucified. He told of the resurrection. He spoke of the ascension to heaven. He quoted the prophetic words of David: "The Lord said to my Lord: 'Sit at my right hand until I make your enemies a footstool for your feet.'" Acts 2:34-35. He concluded by saying, "Therefore let all Israel be assured of this: God has made this Jesus, whom you crucified, both Lord and Christ." Acts 2:36.

What a ringing testimony! Peter drew the proverbial "line in the sand." Everyone was on one side or the other. The issue was simple. Either Christ was recognized and bowed to as Lord or they were God's enemies. There was no middle ground, no room for compromise. The burning question, pressed on hearts by the Holy Spirit's convicting power was simple: "Where does that leave you?"

Well, about 3000 people cried out, "Brothers, what shall we do?" (Verse 37), and were baptized, becoming devoted followers of the one they had crucified. They were filled with gladness and praise, continuing in steadfast fellowship with the apostles and with each other.

Wherever the gospel went it began with, "Jesus Christ is Lord." He was presented as Creator, Savior, Risen and Reigning Lord, Son of God, heir to a throne that would last forever, the one who sustains the universe by his Word, and the Judge before whom all men will one day stand to give account. Hebrews 1, Colossians 1:15-20, Acts 17:31.

In Philippians 2:6-11 Paul tells of the voluntary humiliation of Christ who became obedient even to death on a cross. He continues, "Therefore God exalted him to the highest place and gave him the name that is above every name, that at the name of Jesus every knee should bow, in heaven and on earth and under the earth, and every tongue confess that Jesus Christ is Lord, to the glory of God the Father."

The very foundation, not only of the message, but also of the ministry of proclaiming the gospel is found in the words of Jesus: "All authority in heaven and on earth has been given to me." Matt. 28:18. The world stands in utter opposition to this authority as Jesus himself indicated in a parable when he said, "… his subjects hated him and sent a delegation after him to say, 'We don't want this man to be our king.'" Luke 19:14.

David prophesied of this when he said, "Why do the nations conspire and the peoples plot in vain? The kings of the earth take their stand and the rulers gather together against the Lord and against his Anointed One. 'Let us break their chains,' they say, 'and throw off their fetters.'" Psalm 2:1-3. But their rebellion is in vain. One day every rebel will stand before a great white throne and answer to the very one against whom he has rebelled. Jesus is Lord. Period.

Lord, Lord

Of course, a great deal more could be said about the Lordship of Christ but I can just hear some reader saying, "Well, of course Jesus is Lord; every Church believes that." Do they? Would that they did.

In Luke 6:46, Jesus asked the people, "Why do you call me, 'Lord, Lord,' and do not do what I say?" The issue is not *saying* but *doing*. Jesus illustrated the difference by speaking of two houses, one with a foundation laid on a rock and the other without a foundation but simply built on the ground. One day a flood came and only the one founded upon the rock stood. There is no foundation in simply calling Jesus, "Lord." If He is not actually obeyed what good are mere words?

We see this clearly in Matthew 7. There Jesus spoke of two gates and two ways (13-14). Each way is religious and promises heaven but only one actually leads there. That is the small gate and the narrow way. The wide gate and the broad road lead to destruction. This road attracts "many." Only a "few" find the narrow way. "Many" and "few": it sounds like the majority of professed followers of Jesus are actually deceived and heading for destruction.

Jesus continued by talking about false prophets who would be known by their fruit. What is He talking about? What is the real essential difference between these two gates and ways?

The key is found in verses 21-23 where Jesus says, "Not everyone who says to me, 'Lord, Lord,' will enter the kingdom of heaven, but only he who does the will of my Father who is in heaven. Many will say to me on that day, 'Lord, Lord, did we not prophesy in your name, and in your name drive out demons and perform many miracles?' Then I will tell them plainly, 'I never knew you. Away from me, you evildoers!'"

That is pretty serious language. Here are people who call Jesus, "Lord," and are zealous in religious activity yet are rejected in the end. Why? Jesus calls them "evildoers." The word "evildoers" in the Greek means "lawless ones." These are rebels who have somehow been deluded with the idea that they could simply call Jesus, "Lord," but in actual practice do what *they* wanted to. They weren't doing the will of God at all but their own.

The wide gate and the broad way simply represent all of the false teachings that convey to people the idea that they can go to heaven without actually surrendering to Christ as Lord. They would probably be ready to fight to defend the *doctrine* that Jesus is Lord but in practical reality He is not *their* Lord. Self is on the throne before they go through the wide gate and remains there all the way to the judgment.

What His Lordship Means

Going through the narrow gate means that Jesus who IS Lord becomes MY Lord. The Lordship of Christ is not merely a doctrine or a general principle. It is meant to find practical expression in individual lives. The true follower of Jesus does not belong to himself. His life is not his own to live as he pleases. He has been bought with a price.

He has given up his life, taken up his cross to follow Jesus. He is a servant, a slave to the one who gave all to save him. Even as Jesus lived, he lives, not to do his own will, but to do the will of God. He belongs to another. Self has given up the throne forever. He has died that he might live. One life has been laid down that he might come to possess another, a life untainted by sin, one that will last forever. 1 Cor. 6:19-20. Matt. 16:24-27. Romans 6:3-4. Col. 3:1-4.

I am afraid that churches are filled with people who profess to follow Jesus but who have never truly bowed to him as Lord of their lives — personally. This is a mark of deception. Sometimes even those exposed to the true gospel will somehow delude themselves in this way but more often it is the fault of the so-called "gospel" they embrace. It gives them a false hope. They may even embrace the doctrine of the Lordship of Christ and yet never actually surrender to the Lord himself.

Remember that it is God's *kingdom* we are talking about. That kingdom has a king and the government is upon his shoulders. Isaiah 9:6. He has all authority in heaven and earth. Matt. 28:18. He is the way, the truth and the life. No one comes to the Father except by him. John 14:6. In John 10 Jesus calls himself "the good shepherd," likening his true followers to sheep. In verse 9, He said, "I am the gate; whoever enters through me will be saved. He will come in and go out, and find pasture."

We are either citizens of a lost and perishing world or we are citizens of that kingdom. The riches and benefits of that kingdom are beyond imagining. There are some who preach a "Jesus" who — virtually without condition — opens wide the door to all who merely profess to follow him. But there is simply no way to obtain the benefits of heavenly citizenship without surrendering to the king! No one will ever go around him and get to God. He is not only the king but the very gateway into the kingdom.

Think about it! The very essence of our sin problem is that we are rebels. Any gospel that does not begin with surrender — an end to our rebellion — is no gospel at all. It is deception. That is why the very beginning of Paul's message was simply Christ, and more specifically, that Jesus Christ is Lord. There is no way around that. Men will either reckon with him here in surrender or they will reckon with him there in judgment. Those are the only choices.

To put it another way, God has not given us a religion, but a Person. Our hope lies not in obeying precepts and commandments but in opening our innermost beings — our hearts — to receive that Person for all that he is, and that starts with the fact that he is Lord. Is he your Lord?

Chapter 4

Which Gospel?

In 2 Cor. 11:2-4 we find Paul the apostle greatly concerned for the Corinthian believers. He had poured out his life to bring them the true gospel and to establish them firmly in Christ. But Satan wasn't about to give up on these believers. He sent and inspired religious teachers to undermine what the Lord through Paul had accomplished.

And so Paul wrote, "I am jealous for you with a godly jealousy. I promised you to one husband, to Christ, so that I might present you as a pure virgin to him. But I am afraid that just as Eve was deceived by the serpent's cunning, your minds may somehow be led astray from your sincere and pure devotion to Christ. For if someone comes to you and preaches a Jesus other than the Jesus we preached, or if you receive a different spirit from the one you received, or a different gospel from the one you accepted, you put up with it easily enough."

Satan has filled the world with such teachers and God's people need to know how to recognize the difference. Not every "Jesus" is the real Jesus, the one Paul preached. Not every spirit is of God. Not every gospel is the genuine "good news" that Jesus commanded his disciples to preach among the nations.

We have already pointed out the simplicity of the message God had sent him to proclaim. He expressed the essence of his message as, "Jesus Christ and him crucified." 1 Cor. 2:2. The person and work of Christ was Paul's whole message.

With regard to Christ's person we have pointed to what Paul said in 2 Cor. 4:5 — "For we do not preach ourselves, but Jesus Christ as Lord, and ourselves as your servants for Jesus' sake." Any "gospel" that does not bring people under the lordship of Christ is no gospel at all. At best it puts them on the broad road that leads to destruction. Matt. 7:13.

God's Purpose, Not Ours

We highlighted the fact that the gospel concerns God's purpose and not man's needs and desires. God made us in His image to live in an unbroken relationship based on divine love. But sin entered and the human race fell under the curse of death. Therefore God's purpose in salvation is to call out a people from this broken world in order ultimately to fulfill His original purpose. In the end a pure and holy God will dwell with men and they will be His people. Rev. 21:3.

The true gospel reveals God's provision for lost men and women in order to bring about His ultimate intention. It is Christ-centered. One of the chief marks of deception is when the "gospel" that is preached becomes man-centered instead.

By nature man is focused on this world and this life. His goals and purposes are self-centered. Knowing this, Satan has inspired a great variety of religion that caters to man's natural desires in one way or another.

In John 16:8-11 Jesus spoke of the work of the Holy Spirit in these words: "When he comes, he will convict the world of guilt in regard to sin and righteousness and judgment: in regard to sin, because men do not believe in me; in regard to righteousness, because I am going to the Father, where you can see me no longer; and in regard to judgment, because the prince of this world now stands condemned."

Wherever the true gospel is going forth, the Holy Spirit will be carrying out His work. There will be genuine conviction of sin and hearts will be brought to a place of shame and need before a holy God. Their hearts will be plowed and made ready for the seed of God's word that alone brings eternal life. James 1:18. 1 Peter 1:23-25. There is love, but there is no appeal to the flesh, no flattery in the gospel. It shines an uncompromising light on man's true condition.

It seems that in our day "old-fashioned" truths like man's utter sinfulness and the necessity of the cross and the blood of Christ to cleanse from sin have fallen out of fashion in many places. Other more attractive emphases have taken their place, teachings more apt to attract a crowd. Becoming more "seeker-friendly" is the watchword. Get people in and involved and somewhere along the line get them "saved."

None of that for Paul. Wherever he went he told men the truth about their need and about judgment to come unless they repented. He lifted up God's only provision for their need, not a religion but a Person: Jesus Christ. Christ was presented as the sacrifice who willingly bore the sins of lost men. He was also presented as the very means of their becoming fully saved and made ready for an eternal future with a holy God. All of this was done with the anointing of God's Spirit and the result was that men were genuinely born of that Spirit and made new creatures in Christ.

Listen to Paul's words regarding God and His provision in 1 Cor. 1:30 — "It is because of him that you are in Christ Jesus, who has become for us wisdom from God — that is, our righteousness, holiness and redemption." He expressed the same thing in Col. 1:27 as, "Christ in you, the hope of glory."

Man's Condition

As we have said, man in his sin-darkened condition is totally self-centered, totally focused on his own desires and purposes. He cares nothing for the will of God. Of everything, he asks, "What's in it for me?" He is a willing citizen of this present world — not just the planet we live on — but a spiritual order of things dominated by the darkness of sin and rebellion against our Creator and ruled over by legions of wicked spirits led by Lucifer himself.

This spiritual order is characterized by the things John the apostle describes in 1 John 2:16: "the cravings of sinful man, the lust of his eyes and the boasting of what he has and does." These things come not from God but are rather an abomination to Him. He has decreed that the world — and its desires — will pass away; only the man who does the will of God will live forever. 1 John 2:17.

Because of sin the citizens of this present age live under the shadow of death. No matter what they do in this life death wins in the end. No exceptions. And yet man in his blindness, if left to himself, would live and die and never once think about God. Every natural inclination of his heart is to cling greedily to the very sin that binds him in chains of darkness. He is a slave, a prisoner, unwilling and unable to break free.

It is the mercy of God when He intervenes to cause men even to be aware that He is. And yet the sinfulness of sin is revealed in the fact that most men will readily *choose* darkness even when confronted with light. Jesus brought the light of God's life into the arena of men in a unique way yet he was despised and rejected by most men. They loved their sin and hated Jesus for exposing it. And the worst offenders were the religious folks! How can anything be called the gospel and not confront man's need in a truthful way? The gospel is not about making people feel good about themselves; it is about rescuing them from a hopeless situation.

Before he met Jesus in blinding revelation on the road to Damascus, Saul the Jew was a very religious man. In the eyes of men — and in his own eyes — he was moral, righteous, and upright. It would be easy to see such a man and suppose that all he needs is a little "tune-up," a little "course correction," a little more information. But Paul didn't need a mere "tune-up"; he needed a new engine! And he was headed 180 degrees in the wrong direction! What he considered to be truth was in fact a carefully contrived counterfeit designed to seal him in darkness and send him to hell.

Before he met Jesus, Saul was self-righteous and spiritually confident. In the light of God's glory that shown out from Jesus, Saul's opinion of himself changed. In a moment of time he went from being a self-righteous Pharisee to being the very worst of sinners. 1 Timothy 1:15. That is a pretty radical change!

How many people in our day join churches and profess to follow Jesus without ever becoming aware of just how desperately they need a Savior? If a religious man like Saul needed a radical revolution in his heart how much more do we?

Man's Helplessness

God's word reveals that not only is our need great and our condition dire, we are helpless to *do* anything about it. There is no religion we can practice, no work we can perform, no human effort of any kind that will change our circumstances in the slightest. A man bound in chains and locked in a prison cell is helpless unless someone with a key sets him free. Our bondage to sin and our guilt are so great that our only hope is that mercy will be granted and someone else will do what is necessary to deliver us.

Yet man in his blind pride highly resents any suggestion that he is a helpless undeserving sinner. He compares himself with others and vainly imagines that he is better than most and surely able through his own religious efforts to obtain God's favor. He may well be a candidate for a form of religion that caters to his natural desires in some way yet angrily reject any effort on God's part to show him his true need.

More Than Doctrine

There is one aspect of truth that needs to be emphasized at this point and that is this: we need *more* than even adherence to the correct doctrine concerning man and his need of salvation if God's work is to be accomplished. Sadly it is possible to convert people to the *doctrine* of human depravity and need and yet leave them lost and in their sins.

I have encountered people over the years who were full of pride in the soundness of their doctrine (by their standard, at least!) who nonetheless lack the grace one would expect to see in one who has truly been rescued from the very depravity they profess so strongly to believe in. Orthodox doctrine is not enough.

Paul rightly summed up his message as "Jesus Christ and him crucified" yet he did not stop there. He went on to say, "My message and my preaching were not with wise and persuasive words, but with a demonstration of the Spirit's power, so that your faith might not rest on men's wisdom, but on God's power." 1 Cor. 2:4-5.

The gospel of Jesus Christ is more than mere words, no matter how correct those words may be. As Paul said in Romans 1:16, "… it is the power of God for the salvation of everyone who believes." The gospel involves words but those words accomplish nothing if they are not a vehicle through which God's Spirit directly confronts the hearers. Jesus said of his words that they were "spirit" and "life." John 6:63. Words that do not have spirit and life are just …

Dead Words

Suppose you were trying to form a basketball team. You imagine the kind of player you want to play the position of center. He ought to be at least 6'10" and weigh at least 275 pounds. Someone says, "I know just the man!" He leaves and later returns with a large box. He opens the box and displays a large man, saying, "I found exactly what you are looking for, a man who is 6'10" and weighs 275 pounds." You say, "Well, he is the correct size all right. There's just one problem: he's dead!"

The example is ridiculous, of course, yet there is a lot of religion that is no more effective in terms of eternal things than trying to win a game with that dead basketball player. They have some truth, handed down from generation to generation, but it is dead in terms of spiritual power. The words may convert some minds but the Spirit of God is absent and the hearers never actually come face to face with God.

God's Words

God's words are powerful. Hebrews 4:12 says, "For the word of God is living and active. Sharper than any double-edged sword, it penetrates even to dividing soul and spirit, joints and marrow; it judges the thoughts and attitudes of the heart."

God created all that is by merely speaking. Our words may convey *information* but God's words convey real *power* as well, enough to create galaxies of stars when it pleases Him. The preaching of the gospel is actually intended to be creative as well since one transformed by it is a "new creation." 2 Corinthians 5:17. When a sinner is truly born again it is as much an act of divine creation as it was when God created stars.

In 2 Peter 3:5-7 we find Peter speaking of scoffers at the end of the age: "But they deliberately forget that long ago by God's word the heavens existed and the earth was formed out of water and by water. By these waters also the world of that time was deluged and destroyed. By the same word the present heavens and earth are reserved for fire, being kept for the day of judgment and destruction of ungodly men." God's Word is powerful indeed!

Human Instruments

Those called of God to preach the gospel do not merely **relay information**. That is, God does not simply give them facts to pass on to the minds of their hearers. Rather they are human instruments through which **God Himself speaks**. It is the very Spirit of God that goes out through the words and engages the hearts of the hearers. That is the purpose of the anointing. The anointing transforms mere religious speech into an expression of God Himself capable of imparting life. People do not need to be merely educated; they need to be raised from the dead!

Paul understood the difference. Before stating the central principle of having no other message than Jesus Christ and him crucified he first said, "When I came to you, brothers, I did not come with eloquence or superior wisdom as I proclaimed to you the testimony about God." 1 Corinthians 2:1. He was rightly concerned that he not simply persuade men using human ability but that he rather bring men into direct contact with God in life and power. Paul spoke — but he relied on God's anointing to do the actual work in his hearers.

Religion is full of gifted orators, charismatic personalities, keen intellects, men with natural ability to influence others. But to the extent that ministry is an expression of these human qualities it is worthless to the kingdom of God. Even if the doctrine itself is pure what good is it if it is dead?

Worse than that is when the devil gets involved. He is a great employer of religious men who operate apart from God's Spirit and calling. That is why Paul warned of "another spirit." Just because some kind of spiritual power seems to be in operation does not at all guarantee that the power is of God.

Spirit and Truth

In John 4:24 Jesus said to the woman at the well, "God is spirit, and his worshipers must worship in spirit and in truth." Where God is at work there will always be both spirit **and** truth. Either without the other leaves much room for deception.

It is our job to proclaim the message. It is The Holy Spirit's job to drive that message home to hearts. Earlier we pointed out what Jesus said in John 16:8 — "When he comes, he will convict the world of guilt in regard to sin and righteousness and judgment."

A true knowledge of these things comes only by divine revelation to the heart. It cannot be conveyed by mere words no matter how intellectually brilliant or emotionally charged they may be. Only the Spirit of God can so convince a man deep on the inside of these truths that godly sorrow for sin, true repentance and faith become possible — and then only by God's grace.

Something Drastic Needed

Let's summarize again briefly what the gospel is intended to address. Mankind is hopelessly enslaved by the power of sin and death in a world ruled by wicked spirits of darkness under the leadership of Lucifer. He lives and dies serving "self." God has given him laws to show what righteousness is but those laws also serve to show man what a sinner he is since he has no power or true desire to obey them. If God's original purpose to have a people with whom He can live in harmony and love is to be fulfilled something drastic needs to be done.

But by whom? Man can do nothing to remedy his situation. Thus the gospel reveals, not what WE must do to make ourselves acceptable to God but rather what GOD has done in sending His Son to earth to die on the cross.

The law of God demands that every sinner die. Jesus assumed our guilt and shame and willingly received in himself the full penalty of God's broken law. Justice has been fully upheld. Because of what Jesus did God can remain just and yet cleanse from the guilt of sin, declaring sinners righteous. Romans 3:21-26.

Obtaining the Blessing

But who are those who enter into this blessed state of being accepted by God as righteous? Can a man pray a simple "formula" prayer and be saved? Is it a matter of simply praying the right words? Can a man somehow obtain this blessing yet reserve the right to continue serving self and sin? Can he remain lord of his own life and yet "accept" Jesus? Will Jesus share the throne of the heart with "self"?

Of course the answer to these questions is a resounding "no"! And yet the honest answer in many places in our day would have to be "yes." "That's all there is to it. Just pray a little prayer accepting Jesus. It's simple."

Well, it is true that the gospel is indeed simple — but it is not EASY. It is not easy because it demands that we bow in surrender to the Lordship of Christ, assuming our rightful place as penitent sinners in need of mercy. As we have said, only the active work of the Holy Spirit can accomplish this.

If this is somehow bypassed — and it is in many places in our day — then deception has taken root. The Jesus who offers salvation without surrender is not the Jesus Paul preached. It is another Jesus who preaches the wide gate that many enter only to be destroyed in the end.

If Satan is to deceive he must — for many at least — seem to uphold the truth of man's need of salvation and yet carefully avoid the kind of encounter with God that produces new creatures in Christ. If he can convince men that they are saved when they are not then he is free to build great religious movements that deceive many.

Chapter 5

Truly Born Again: What Now?

Assuming, then, that men have indeed experienced the miracle of the new birth, what then? What is this thing called the Christian life about? We know what men seek in this world but what is it that God seeks? What is His purpose in calling us to continue living in such a broken world? And how is that purpose to be fulfilled?

Surely one of the favorite scriptures of believers down through the ages has been Romans 8:28 — "And we know that in all things God works for the good of those who love him, who have been called according to his purpose." This wonderful verse reminds us that everything that happens to God's people is part of a divine plan, a plan that is meaningful, purposeful, and that God's purpose for us results in our good.

But what is that purpose? Verse 29 continues the thought: "For those God foreknew he also predestined to be conformed to the likeness of his Son, that he might be the firstborn among many brothers." Here we see God's purpose to produce a great family of "sons," each of them having been made like Jesus. That would, of course, make Jesus the firstborn, the pattern. The focus of God's purpose therefore is the **character** of His children.

God's Work

But we also see that God's purpose is fulfilled by the power and effort of God Himself. Verse 30 continues, "And those he predestined, he also called; those he called, he also justified; those he justified, he also glorified." Who did all this? HE did. It can happen no other way. Every aspect of salvation is supernatural from beginning to end.

Philippians 2:12-13 says, "...continue to work out your salvation with fear and trembling, for it is God who works in you to will and to act according to his good purpose." This scripture reveals both God's role and ours in the process. We have our part but that part is one of cooperation with something God does. It is a place of submission to *His* will and purpose rather than one in which we try to get God to fulfill *our* plans and dreams.

In the first place we are to "work **out**" our salvation. If we are to "work **out**" our salvation it must be "**in**" in the first place! That is, God must first do His supernatural work **in us** before there is something within that can even *be* worked out. You can't pump water out of an empty well.

Both the ability and even the desire for everything that fulfills God's purpose in us comes from Him alone. We are as helpless in ourselves to live for God as we are to save ourselves in the first place. That's why it is called *salvation*!

Created to Be Like God

Paul expresses the same truth in Ephesians 4:22-24 in these words: "You were taught, with regard to your former way of life, to put off your old self, which is being corrupted by its deceitful desires; to be made new in the attitude of your minds; and to put on the new self, created to be like God in true righteousness and holiness." We see our responsibility yet the "new self" we are to "put on" is **created**. That sounds pretty supernatural to me!

Notice the language in that scripture: "created to be like God." What an amazing thought! How utterly beyond our ability such a thing is. Here we see another expression of the fact that salvation is an act of creation. Can you create yourself? Does anyone have the power to produce what God is after by any kind of human effort?

But exactly how does this relate to Paul's message, "Jesus Christ and him crucified"? Look back again at 1 Corinthians 1:30. There we read, "It is because of him that you are in Christ Jesus, who has become for us wisdom from God—that is, our righteousness, holiness and redemption."

The Centrality of Christ

The first "him" is God Himself. It is a result of **His work** that we are "in Christ Jesus" at all. Yet look at all that Christ Jesus has "become" for us: wisdom, righteousness, holiness and redemption." That is a pretty good description of everything involved in fulfilling His purpose in making us like Christ!

Read the writings of Paul and you will see everywhere just how central the person and work of Christ is to living for God and becoming what He has planned. In salvation not only are my sins borne by Christ but I receive His righteousness as my own. I am accepted by God just as much as He is! 2 Corinthians 5:21, Ephesians 1:3-8. God fully accepts His Son and since I am **IN** Him that includes me as well! To put it crudely, if you give someone a box they receive not only the box but also whatever is **in** it.

How can I put off my old self? Romans 6 tells us that when Christ died, we died. His death becomes *our* death when we are united to him in salvation. Whether I understand it fully or not I have the right to "reckon" or count myself to have died based on the **fact** of what God has done for me when Jesus died.

In the same way those united with Christ were there in him when He rose from the dead to a new life. The life He had in his resurrection is the very same life we receive when we are born of God. What Christ accomplished in his death, burial, and resurrection is the very foundation for living for God.

More than that, we pointed out earlier that our hope of glory is Christ in us (Colossians 1:27). He does not merely tell us how to live but He comes in by the Spirit to indwell us and live out his life in us. As A.B. Simpson wrote in his hymn long ago, "He Who overcame on Calvary overcomes again in you and me. Hallelujah, Jesus gives the victory."

As Paul said in Galatians 2:20, "I have been crucified with Christ and I no longer live, but Christ lives in me. The life I live in the body, I live by faith in the Son of God, who loved me and gave himself for me." The Greek says the faith **of** the Son of God. When Christ comes in He brings his faith with him!

Christ is the center of everything. No wonder Paul summarized his message as he did. It is fine to teach God's wisdom regarding relationships, overcoming sin, giving, ministry, etc. but if any of these things are divorced from the supernatural foundation of Christ in us then they become mere principles, rules to live by, dependent upon human ability, mere religion. What is left is a "form of godliness" that **denies** its power (2 Timothy 3:5). That sounds like a pretty good way to describe **deception**. It may look good but it isn't real.

A Matter of Family

One of the clearest passages in the scriptures that shows just how connected every aspect of salvation is to the person and work of Christ is in Romans 5. Paul makes a comparison between Adam and Christ showing that what each did was passed to his descendants.

For example in verse 19 Paul writes, "For just as through the disobedience of the one man the many were made sinners, so also through the obedience of the one man the many will be made righteous." How did we become sinners? Adam disobeyed and he became the father of a family of sinners, all mankind. What he did was passed down to us all and our actions prove it.

In the same way those born into Christ's family inherit the result of his obedience and partake of his righteousness. As Paul said in verse 17, "For if, by the trespass of the one man, death reigned through that one man, how much more will those who receive God's abundant provision of grace and of the gift of righteousness reign in life through the one man, Jesus Christ."

What Jesus did on our behalf is the fountain and source of everything God has for us. What else is there to preach? Of course there is a need for teaching on the various aspects of the *outworking* of our salvation as it applies to living here but it all flows from him. That is why Colossians 2:10 tells us that we are "complete in him" (KJV).

That is why Paul speaks as he does in the beginning of chapter 3 (verses 1-3): "Since, then, you have been raised with Christ, set your hearts on things above, where Christ is seated at the right hand of God. Set your minds on things above, not on earthly things. For you died, and your life is now hidden with Christ in God. When Christ, who is your life, appears, then you also will appear with him in glory."

Anything short of this misses the mark and reflects the effort of the enemy to deceive. May God grant grace that His message may be boldly proclaimed, that Christ and Christ alone may be lifted up as the only hope of mankind. May we humbly submit to our Heavenly Father, the Master Craftsman, as He patiently and surely takes that which was ruined by sin and transforms it into something eternal and beautiful. To Him be glory and praise forever and ever!

Chapter 6

What Spirit?

To this point we have briefly explored two particular areas of truth in an attempt to shine a light on ways in which Satan has sought to hinder God's work with deception. The more we understand the true nature of what God is after the better equipped we will be to recognize Satan's counterfeits.

The first area concerns *Christ as the Head*. The headship of Christ means that He literally runs things. It means that He is recognized, looked to, depended upon, submitted to in the day to day life of His church. He is no mere figurehead, a remote monarch whose name is used to sanctify the religious efforts of men. In reality, most religion is run by men. All too often these men are inspired by demons — even where the *doctrine* of Christ's headship is acknowledged.

The second area concerns *Christ as the Message*. Every aspect of truth is centered in the *person* of Jesus Christ. Paul summed up his message in these simple words: "Jesus Christ and him crucified." 1 Corinthians 2:2. Where Christ is not the message, something else is. It's that simple.

The Life

But there is a third area of truth that needs emphasizing: it is simply *Christ as the Life*. Christ is more than the head, more than the message: He is literally the life of His church. Remember Paul's warning in 2 Cor. 11:5 about another Jesus and a different gospel? He also warned us in the same verse about a "different" spirit. Not every spirit in professing Christendom is of God — to say the least!

What is it that distinguishes a fellowship of true followers of Jesus from everyone else? Is it their beliefs? their religious practices? their code of ethics? No! It comes down to one thing: it is the living presence of Christ who has himself become the very source of the life they share. Everything else is mere religion. Of course this truth is very intertwined with the others mentioned yet I believe it needs to be explored in its own right.

In every group claiming to follow Christ there is some sort of spirit that prevails, that gives it life, and that defines its character. We tend to see and judge by external things such as doctrines, styles of worship, denominational affiliation, and the like but God judges by the spirit. It is not the externals that matter most but the spirit that is behind those externals. For example, what is called "worship" may be soulish and emotional or it may be a genuine expression of God's Spirit. The same is true of preaching — and every other aspect of church life.

Religious Culture

Religious groups tend to have their own "cultures," if you will, shared beliefs and practices that distinguish them from others. Sometimes this culture reflects the collective personalities of the members but more often it reflects the preferences of some dominant personality or personalities. If there is a denominational affiliation it probably reflects that as well. For example, a church that is "Baptist" in its tradition and culture will probably look and feel very different from one that is "Pentecostal." The same could be said of any of the "labels" by which we identify different brands of churches.

The tendency for those seeking spiritual fellowship therefore usually involves finding a place where the culture most closely matches the individual's own religious ideas and preferences. Very few seek God with an honest and willing heart. How often over the years have we seen someone begin to visit one of our assemblies and show real interest — and even enthusiasm — for awhile. Then somewhere along the line they drift away or are suddenly offended over some issue and leave. Why?

What really happens is that they come with their own ready-made religious "measuring stick." They use this measuring stick to evaluate what they see and hear. Everything is fine until they run into something that doesn't conform to what they already "know" to be true. They are not really seeking truth with an honest heart but their own preferred brand of religion — and we don't measure up to their standard! God can inspire a message that opens up the Word with great clarity and anointing and they will be completely deaf to it because it isn't what they are used to and looking for.

Their religion has truly been reduced to a religious "culture" that they happen to prefer. The devil himself could be the true inspiration behind a particular group and they wouldn't know the difference as long as it conforms to their ideas of how things should be. Sadly, what I have just described characterizes the great majority of professed followers of Christ.

A Form

In 1 Tim. 4:1 Paul warned Timothy, "The Spirit clearly says that in later times some will abandon the faith and follow deceiving spirits and things taught by demons." In 2 Tim. 3:1 Paul warns that "there will be terrible times in the last days." He describes many characteristics that will be manifest in people but one in verse five stands out: "having a form of godliness but denying its power."

If you read the other things that Paul lists this almost seems out of place, yet it isn't. With most of the other characteristics the evil is pretty obvious: "unholy," "without love," "without self-control," "brutal," "treacherous," and the like. However a "form of godliness" may be the most deadly thing on the list. Why? Because outwardly it looks good. It appears to uphold righteousness and godliness. The problem is that it merely *appears* to. Something demonic is really behind it. How do we know? Because the "power" that belongs to true godliness is *denied*.

If you want a picture of what Paul meant just look back at the religious leaders Jesus had to contend with. He would visit their synagogues and it wouldn't be long before the life and power that was in Him would expose the emptiness of their particular form of "godliness" and He would be rejected. On at least one occasion they even tried to kill Him. Luke 4. They loved their religious form — as long as the living God wasn't involved — as long as His actual power and presence didn't expose their true condition. Their supposed "form of godliness" was actually a cover for the dominion of demons who held the people captive in terrible darkness and deception. When the light that was in Jesus threatened that darkness the demons were quick to stir up all manner of anger and opposition in the people. The real question with any group is simple: What spirit is there?

The Role of Ministry

The churches we read about in the New Testament were founded as Paul and others went forth in the power of the Holy Spirit and proclaimed the message of Jesus Christ. Those who received the message were brought together and taught and churches were born. They were defined by their shared faith and life.

As we have said, the ministry of the Word of God is more than the mere conveyance of correct ideas. It is literally the vehicle by which God's Spirit enters receptive hearts and imparts life. Put another way, God actually speaks to the people through the lips of the human vessel. Yet this does not mean that the vessel is a mere robot or puppet. Both God and man are engaged in the ministry effort but to the extent the vessel is called and yielded to God the inspiration is divine and the very life of God is ministered to the hearers through the words. 2 Corinthians 3:3-6, Colossians 1:29. 1 Corinthians 2:1-5.

Understandably over time the ministry will define the life of a given church. Where God is present, those whose hearts He has opened will hear His voice, be drawn to Christ, and begin to be changed. This change is far deeper than mere outward things. It is much more than just conformity to a particular religious standard. Rather, the very Spirit of God is imparted to the people and they are changed from the inside out. Those whose hearts are blinded by sin and religion tend to go their own way at some point because they have a different spirit.

On the other hand, what is produced where the ministry is *not* truly sent and anointed by God? What about ministry that is characterized by human ability, pride, ambition, religious zeal, tradition, a sectarian spirit, etc.? What kind of church would result from that? Would the life and blessing of God flow freely in the lives of the people? Would sinners be drawn to their light? Would that kind of ministry impart the very life of Christ to the people?

If not, what *would* be imparted? There are only two options: it is either Christ himself or something that is utterly opposed to Him. The Bible calls such a spirit "antichrist" because it is a spirit that is *against* Christ. The religious life in such a place might even look good outwardly but what would happen if Christ himself showed up? When Paul spoke of a form of godliness that *denies* the power he meant that there was a built-in *opposition* to God's presence and power. A mere "form" of godliness is not neutral. In fact, it *hates* Christ, regardless of appearances.

What do you think would happen in most modern churches if Paul the Apostle were suddenly to become the pastor?! I'm afraid in most places it would be war! The result would be similar to the reception Jesus received in the synagogues of His day. People would be fuming, "We don't do things that way!" "You're violating our traditions!" "How *dare* you suggest that there is something wrong with us!"

I believe there are places where such a ministry would provoke true repentance in at least some of the people but in far more places they would be quick to show Paul the door. Their outward behavior might be somewhat more refined than that of the religious folks of Jesus' day but their true spirit would be just the same towards Paul as it was in those who crucified Jesus.

What is the Church?
What is the church anyway? What did God have in mind? What is it that Christ promised to build when He said, "I will build my church"? Matt. 16:18. I believe that if we better understand God's intent with respect to the church then it will be easier to recognize the counterfeits that abound. As we consider this it is surely important to acknowledge that at best even true expressions of the church are typically in a very immature state and need to grow — the Corinthian church,

for example. They did not lack "any spiritual gift" (1 Corinthians 1:7) yet look at the many problems they had! However, there is a fundamental difference between an immature church where Christ lives and one ruled by another spirit. They are on two different tracks headed in opposite directions.

Father and Son

I believe the correct starting point for understanding the nature of the church is to first understand something about the Father and His Son. I'm not talking about something deep and theological but rather a simple scriptural picture of their relationship. The relationship they enjoyed during our Savior's time on earth is a picture of God's plan for His people as well.

Phil. 2:6-7 speaks of Christ, "who, although He existed in the form of God, did not regard equality with God a thing to be grasped, but emptied Himself, taking the form of a bond-servant, and being made in the likeness of men." (NASU.) There was a drastic change between heaven and earth. Between the "form of God" and the "likeness of men" there was an *emptying*. He remained *Who* He was; however, the *what* changed. He had become a man.

In His prayer in John 17 Jesus said, "I have brought you glory on earth by completing the work you gave me to do. And now, Father, glorify me in your presence with the glory I had with you before the world began." (Verses 4-5). Here again we see a contrast drawn between Christ's glory before

He came to earth and what He was on earth. And having completed the work He had been sent to do He expected to reclaim the glory He had laid aside.

John 1 begins with these familiar words in the first three verses: "In the beginning was the Word, and the Word was with God, and the Word was God. He was with God in the beginning. Through him all things were made; without him nothing was made that has been made." Here again we catch a glimpse of what Christ was before coming to earth.

Also He is called "the Word," the very expression of the Father. Col. 1:15 says of Him, "He is the image of the invisible God…." Heb. 1:3 says, "The Son is the radiance of God's glory and the exact representation of his being…." See also John 1:18. If you want to know what God is like, look at Jesus.

The Earthly Life of Jesus

Then John 1:14 adds these words: "The Word became flesh and made his dwelling among us. We have seen his glory, the glory of the One and Only, who came from the Father, full of grace and truth." Though He had been so great and glorious, yet to fulfill His Father's plan He willingly laid aside His former glory and actually "became flesh"! How amazing is that!

Despite who He was and what He had been before, Jesus lived his earthly life as a man. He lived in complete dependence upon His Father. In John 5:19 Jesus said, "I tell you the truth, the Son can do nothing by himself; he can do only what he sees his Father doing, because whatever the

Father does the Son also does." He reiterates the same thought in verse 30: "By myself I can do nothing; I judge only as I hear, and my judgment is just, for I seek not to please myself but him who sent me."

Please note that Jesus did *not* say, "I *choose* to do nothing by myself." Rather He said, "By myself I *can* do nothing." The *choice* was to come to earth in the first place. Once here He did not possess the *ability* in Himself to do the wonderful things He did. Remember, He had *emptied* Himself. This is little understood. It is supposed by some that because He was the Son of God that He had power to do anything He wanted and just voluntarily refrained from using that power apart from His Father's will. No! He was not an actor. He ministered upon earth as a Spirit-filled man. His dependence upon God was genuine.

Speaking of the ministry of Jesus, John the Baptist said, "For the one whom God has sent speaks the words of God, for God gives the Spirit without limit. The Father loves the Son and has placed everything in his hands." John 3:34-35. How was Jesus able to speak God's words? He was able because God gave Him the Spirit without limit.

Earlier John had testified, "I saw the Spirit come down from heaven as a dove and remain on him. I would not have known him, except that the one who sent me to baptize with water told me, 'The man on whom you see the Spirit come down and remain is he who will baptize with the Holy Spirit.' I have seen and I testify that this is the Son of God." John 1:32-34. Amazing! Until the Spirit came upon him Jesus appeared to be just another man coming to John for baptism! (We should note that John himself had an inner witness as to who Jesus was as he approached the water — John 1:29, Matt. 4:13-15 — but the decisive, divinely promised witness to John was the coming of the Spirit upon Jesus.)

Jesus' Baptism

The baptism of Jesus marked a radical change in the His earthly life. Before that He was just a fine Jewish boy growing up in Nazareth, attending the synagogue, working as a carpenter. There are religious myths that picture Him performing miracles as a child but they are not so. If He had His own power why did He need the anointing of the Holy Spirit? Why did not the Father simply say, "It's time. Show them what you can do"?

At one point in His ministry Jesus was performing many miracles and drawing great crowds yet his own brothers didn't believe in Him! John 7:3-5. That surely testifies to the fact that there was nothing that remarkable about Him prior to the Jordan River experience. By the way — I mentioned earlier about the synagogue where the people tried to kill Him — that synagogue was in Nazareth, the home town of Jesus! The people there had known Him His whole life. Luke tells us that he went to the synagogue "as was his custom." There was nothing unusual in His standing up to read either. He had no doubt done it many times before. But something was dramatically different this time. He spoke with the power of God's Spirit. The Spirit confronted their spiritual condition and they reacted with murderous rage.

Why had He never provoked such a reaction before? Was it because Jesus had simply chosen to *hide* His power? No! He had no power for ministry apart from the anointing granted Him from above. Just before this Jesus had spent 40 days in the wilderness being tempted by the devil following His baptism. Then Luke says, "Jesus returned to Galilee in the power of the Spirit, and news about him spread through the whole countryside." Luke 4:14. The impartation of the Spirit at baptism and the wilderness testing set the stage for God's power to be manifest in His earthly ministry.

The disciples were witness to many amazing things as they traveled about with Jesus. They saw Him heal the sick, raise dead people, cast out demons, multiply food, walk on water. Three of them had even seen Him shine like the sun when He was transfigured on the mountain. As His ministry on earth drew to a close Jesus revealed to them how all this had come about.

He had often spoken of His Father and so in John 14:8 we read, "Philip said, 'Lord, show us the Father and that will be enough for us.'" In verses 9-10 the record continues, "Jesus answered: 'Don't you know me, Philip, even after I have been among you such a long time? Anyone who has seen me has seen the Father. How can you say, "Show us the Father"? Don't you believe that I am in the Father, and that the Father is in me? The words I say to you are not just my own. Rather, it is the Father, living in me, who is doing his work.'"

How did Jesus do such amazing things? His relationship with the Father was such that it was really the Father *living in Him* that was doing the work. Note also that the work itself was "his" — that is, the Father's — work. In other words Jesus the man was a willing vessel in whom the Father lived and through whom the Father carried out *His* work. The power did not come from Jesus but from the Father. Remember how He had said, "By myself I can do nothing."

The Divine Relationship

Note that in the scripture cited above Jesus also spoke of this divine relationship in these words: "I am in the Father, and ... the Father is in me." These words describe a oneness not only in purpose and action but of *being itself*. It reminds us of Jesus' words in John 15 about the vine and branches. A vine and its branches have a living connection and share the same life. The vine doesn't send a letter to the branch telling it to produce fruit! Fruit is the result of the life that is in the vine flowing into the branch and producing fruit according to the nature of that life. Divine life produces divine fruit and so it was with Jesus. The relationship was so perfect that Jesus was able to say in John 10:30, "I and the Father are one."

God's plan for us is of the same sort. Of course, the passage about the vine and branches actually describes the relationship between Christ and His disciples. In Jesus' prayer in John 17 He said, "Holy Father, protect them by the power of your name — the name you gave me — so that they may be one as we are one." John 17:11. One way to express the meaning behind the name we have come to know as Jesus is "God saves." Note that this name is spoken of by Jesus as "*your* name." The name "Jesus" belonged to the Father before it was given to the Son! It speaks of the very character and purpose of the Father Himself expressed in the Son He sent to save us. Thus His Son came to bear that name, the name that is above every name! Phil. 2:9-11.

We see in this that the underlying power in our salvation comes from the very being of our heavenly Father Himself. I'm so glad that He is not depending upon some power in me for I have none. I am completely helpless apart from a power outside myself — divine power — and that is the hope of the gospel. But note the particular result of that saving power that Jesus focused on in His prayer: "that they may be one as we are one." God desires the same oneness for us that He and His Son enjoyed! Surely only divine power could accomplish such a thing. I am quite sure that when God's family enjoys the beautiful new creation He has promised all of the things that divide us here will be long gone. May we have the heart and the vision to desire more of that unity down here, not an artificial relationship brought about by men, but a true unity based on God's Spirit.

We Are Included

But there is more. Listen to Jesus' prayer in John 17:20-23, noting that we are included: "My prayer is not for them alone. I pray also for those who will believe in me through their message, that all of them may be one, Father, just as you are in me and I am in you. May they also be in us so that the world may believe that you have sent me. I have given them the glory that you gave me, that they may be one as we are one: I in them and you in me. May they be brought to complete unity to let the world know that you sent me and have loved them even as you have loved me."

Jesus prays for our unity, the kind described in the words, "just as you are in me and I am in you." But it is more than a unity with one another God seeks. Jesus also said, "May they also be in us...." This is an extension of the unity between Father and Son. Now it becomes "I in them and you in me." The family grows yet it is more than a family. There is a oneness of being since *all share the same life*, the very life of God. In John 14:20 Jesus spoke of a day when His followers would "realize that I am in my Father, and you are in me, and I am in you."

This truth lends deeper meaning to the words of Jesus when He appeared to his disciples in a locked room after the resurrection. In John 20:21 He said, "Peace be with you! As the Father has sent me, I am sending you." There is more than a simple commission in these words. How, in fact, did the Father send the Son? Did He simply give Him instructions and then stand back, leaving Jesus to His own resources? No, of course not! It was the Father's own Spirit, His own power, His own work that was manifest in the Son. Jesus provided a surrendered human vessel; His Father provided the rest. God's plan for His church is no different. It is either Christ in us or it is us practicing empty religion.

Three Comings of Christ

It is widely understood and believed that Christ came to earth about 2000 years ago to live among us, die for our sins, rise again, and return to a place of enthronement in heaven. It is also widely believed that Christ will one day come again as He promised and as the angels testified when He was taken up to heaven before the disciples. Acts 1:10-11. But there is another coming that is little understood.

This coming is described in various ways and I will just give you what the scriptures say without trying to explain it all. While speaking of the coming of the Counselor, the Spirit of truth Jesus said this: "I will not leave you as orphans; I will come to you." John 14:18. Note His words: "*I will come* ...." This clearly wasn't referring to His first coming since He was already there speaking to them! And in the context He wasn't speaking of the "second coming" either. What coming is He talking about?

One thing that is important to note is that this coming is "to you." Listen to what else Jesus said on the heels of this: "Before long, the world will not see me anymore, but you will see me. Because I live, you also will live. On that day you will realize that I am in my Father, and you are in me, and I am in you. Whoever has my commands and obeys them, he is the one who loves me. He who loves me will be loved by my Father, and I too will love him and show myself to him." John 14:19-21.

There are many things worth noting here. It should be obvious that this "coming" does not refer to either what we call the "incarnation" or to the "second coming." This is something different. Jesus promised to "come" *to the disciples*. He said that the world would not see Him but that the disciples would. He promised to make Himself known in a special way to them in this coming. It is in the middle of this passage that Jesus said, "I am in my Father, and you are in me, and I am in you." That was to be the result of the "coming" of which He spoke. In verse 28 He reiterates this by saying, "I am going away and I am coming back to you."

In Acts 1:4-5 we find Jesus instructing the disciples just before He returned to heaven in these oft-quoted words: "Do not leave Jerusalem, but wait for the gift my Father promised, which you have heard me speak about. For John baptized with water, but in a few days you will be baptized with the Holy Spirit." Despite walking with Jesus for more than 3 years they were not ready for ministry. Jesus promised to send them as He had been sent by the Father. Prior to His baptism in the Jordan Jesus was not equipped either.

There is a parallel between Jesus' baptism and Pentecost. His baptism marked the point at which Jesus was empowered for His work. What happened can be scripturally described as the Holy Spirit coming upon Him. It can also be described as the Father coming to live IN Him based on His words in John 14:10. Jesus, the human vessel, was empowered for a divine mission because God came to live in Him.

At Pentecost we see the Spirit coming upon the apostles with great demonstration and power. But based on the words of Jesus this can also be understood as Christ coming to live — in spirit form — *in* His church. Remember Jesus had used the words "before long" to describe His coming "to them." Now He had come. The same One that had walked among men as Jesus of Nazareth had returned to walk among men once more in the apostles — and by extension, in all who believe. Peter's words were, "Repent and be baptized, every one of you, in the name of Jesus Christ for the forgiveness of your sins. And you will receive the gift of the Holy Spirit. The promise is for you and your children and for all who are far off — for all whom the Lord our God will call." Acts 2:38-39.

Christ's Body

The church is Christ's body. (See Eph. 1:23 and many other scriptures.) At the Jordan the Father came to live in His body, Jesus. At Pentecost, the risen exalted Christ came to live in His body, the church. The apostles were transformed from ordinary men to mighty servants of God. The fruit of Christ's presence was quickly apparent in the power expressed in Peter's message and in the life of the church that resulted. There was an unprecedented unity, love and power among the believers that wonderfully demonstrated God's plan and purpose.

We see these truths reflected in the writings of John the Apostle in his first letter. In 1 John 1:1-4 we read, "That which was from the beginning, which we have heard, which we have seen with our eyes, which we have looked at and our hands have touched — this we proclaim concerning the Word of life. The life appeared; we have seen it and testify to it, and we proclaim to you the eternal life, which was with the Father and has appeared to us. We proclaim to you what we have seen and heard, so that you also may have fellowship with us. And our fellowship is with the Father and with his Son, Jesus Christ." John wrote of a "fellowship" — a *relationship* — that existed involving the Father, his Son, the apostles, and now the believers to whom John was writing.

In 1 John 4:13-14 John says, "We know that we live in him and he in us, because he has given us of his Spirit." The Spirit of God — His very being — is the life we share in Christ, the very foundation of the relationship of which John speaks. In 1 John 4:15 we read, "If anyone acknowledges that Jesus is the Son of God, God lives in him and he in God." In the next verse John says, "God is love. Whoever lives in love lives in God, and God in him." Divine life residing in and expressing itself through human vessels lies at the heart of the church Jesus died and rose again to bring forth.

Many Spirits

But John is well aware that among those who profess to follow Jesus there are those who have other spirits and not the Spirit of God. And so in 1 John 4:1 he says, "Dear friends, do not believe every spirit, but test the spirits to see whether they are from God, because many false prophets have gone out into the world." This is certainly in agreement with Paul's warnings of deception and a form of godliness.

But the test John proposes is very interesting. In verses 2 and 3 he continues, "This is how you can recognize the Spirit of God: Every spirit that acknowledges that Jesus Christ has come in the flesh is from God, but every spirit that does not acknowledge Jesus is not from God. This is the spirit of the antichrist, which you have heard is coming and even now is already in the world."

Christ Come in the Flesh

There is more to this test than one might think. John does **not** say, "every spirit that acknowledges that Jesus Christ **did come** in the flesh is from God." He says, "every spirit that acknowledges that Jesus Christ **has come** in the flesh is from God." There is a profound difference between "did come" and "has come."

To say that Christ "did come" or that He "came" would be to refer to something completely in the past, namely that He **was** a flesh and blood man known as Jesus of Nazareth. But John said, "has come." What is he saying? To say that someone "has come" is the same as saying that someone "is here now"! The "coming" John is speaking of is the same one Jesus talked about in John 14. John heard those words with his own ears. He experienced that coming on the day of Pentecost. But Pentecost wasn't the end of it. John is saying to his readers that Christ not only came then but that **He is still here**.

But there's more. Not only is Christ still here as a result of this coming; He is here "**in the flesh**"! Think about it. When Jesus walked among men the "word" had become flesh. He was the expression of God in flesh. God lived in the flesh of Jesus and in that way walked among men. But the exalted Christ also has a body. His body — and thus His flesh — is the true church composed of all who have been truly born of God's Spirit. He came at Pentecost to inhabit His body — and He still lives in it.

Religious Spirits

There are many religious spirits that don't mind talking about Christ and claiming to serve Christ — as long as it is "Christ in the sky" or a Christ that has some special private relationship with them. But there is something about a religious spirit that is self-willed and independent. It may even acknowledge the doctrine of Christ's incarnation but the idea that He is present in a people today is something else.

Let's be plain. When I say "religious spirit" I am referring to a demon, an emissary of Satan, a very real spiritual being whose specialty is promoting some form of religion that lacks — and bitterly opposes — the actual living presence and power of Christ. Don't kid yourself. Religious spirits come in all "flavors." There are demons actively promoting virtually *every* form of Christianity so long as Christ is absent.

Christ in a people makes those people something unique. It is not that the people themselves are anything but the One who lives in them is the Lord of heaven. Those in whom He lives share not only His life but a mutual responsibility and a mutual submission to one another. The Christ in them binds them together in a supernatural unity. There is an interdependence whereby all benefit from the measure of Christ in each individual member. The church was never meant to be a kind of coalition of independent spirits each feeling free to do "his own thing."

Religious spirits have sort of a "private Christ" that in practice allows them to be a law unto themselves. Jesus spoke of a situation in which a man has sinned against his brother and has also rejected the testimony of two or three that have tried to help him. In Matt. 18:17 Jesus went on to say, "If he refuses to listen to them, tell it to the church; and if he refuses to listen even to the church, treat him as you would a pagan or a tax collector." That is a pretty clear manifestation of the kind of spirit that refuses to acknowledge Christ "come in the flesh."

What God has designed is that His people walk together in love and recognize not only the Christ who reigns above, but *the Christ who lives in His people*. The One I serve, who is in me, is in my brother also. He came not only to save individuals but that we might be joined one to another. Speaking of Jesus, Paul said in Eph. 2:21-22, "In him the whole building is joined together and rises to become a holy temple in the Lord. And in him you too are being built together to become a dwelling in which God lives by his Spirit."

John is not shy about identifying the kind of spirit that refuses to recognize the Christ who lives in the flesh today. In 1 John 4:3 he says, "This is the spirit of the antichrist, which you have heard is coming and *even now is already in the world.*" Thus we see two very different spirits at work in those who profess to follow Jesus: one is the Spirit of Christ; the other is the spirit of antichrist.

Of course John is writing to genuine followers of Christ, a people in whom Christ truly lived. And so he continues in 1 John 4:5-6, "They are from the world and therefore speak from the viewpoint of the world, and the world listens to them. We are from God, and whoever knows God listens to us; but whoever is not from God does not listen to us. This is how we recognize the Spirit of truth and the spirit of falsehood."

Notice the clear connection between being "from God" and recognizing the Christ who lives in His people.

We see this principle also in 1 John 2:18-19 where John had written, "Dear children, this is the last hour; and as you have heard that the antichrist is coming, even now many antichrists have come. This is how we know it is the last hour. They went out from us, but they did not really belong to us. For if they had belonged to us, they would have remained with us; but their going showed that none of them belonged to us."

Two different spirits, each appearing to follow Christ, yet one **is** Christ and the other is actually antichrist. Truly we must not naively believe every spirit. We need God's help if we are to tell the difference. Don't be afraid. He *will* help those who truly want Him!

Chapter 7

Symptoms of Religious Spirits at Work

Let's note once again the words of Jesus to the woman at the well recorded in John 4:23-24 —

"Yet a time is coming and has now come when the true worshipers will worship the Father in spirit and truth, for they are the kind of worshipers the Father seeks. God is spirit, and his worshipers must worship in spirit and in truth."

A key word there is the word "and." There is a safety and balance in Jesus' words and Satan ever seeks to undermine that balance that he might deceive. The pursuit of "truth" apart from God's Spirit results in anything from dead truth to outright falsehood. The pursuit of "spirit" apart from the anchor of truth is a wide open door for delusion. These pursuits tend to appeal to different types of people.

Demon spirits that operate in religion are as varied as those they seek to deceive. Since people differ greatly in their temperament and makeup there is no single approach that the kingdom of darkness can use with everyone. 1 Cor. 1:22 refers to two different types of people in these words: "Jews demand miraculous signs and Greeks look for wisdom." Evidently these were general characteristics of those particular groups but the characteristics noted obviously are not confined to those groups.

The one kind leans strongly toward the "spirit" side of things, emphasizing experience over doctrine, seeking a religion they can feel in some manner, one validated by their earthly senses. The other leans toward the "truth" side, seeking a religion they can understand, and trusting in the power of their minds to seek out and discover truth. Each is in reality a form of unbelief, demanding that God subject Himself to their judgment and approval and meet them on *their* terms.

"Greeks"

Many are the spirits that are at work among the "Greeks" of our world. All spirits need to do to deceive is to encourage such men to deify, to make a god out of, their own intellects. Their own minds become, to them, the highest authority. In their pride, they believe themselves capable of sitting in judgment of anything claiming to be truth, all the while looking down on those they consider to be more ignorant than they are. They specially despise the "I feel it, therefore it must be so" folks, believing them to be easily fooled, yet not realizing they are equally vulnerable.

Spirits know full well that the things of God cannot be discovered through man's intellect so they seize the opportunity afforded by the pride of man's fallen nature to send him on the proverbial "wild goose chase" in one form or another. It matters little what direction that "chase" takes so long as it leads away from the One who IS truth.

There is nothing outside of the person of Jesus Christ that can rightly be called "truth." John 14:6. In Col. 2:3 Paul speaks of Christ, "in whom are hidden all the treasures of wisdom and knowledge." Men acquire all kinds of earthly knowledge in many fields of study but it is all meaningless apart from Christ. That kind of "knowledge" puffs men up with pride — and leads nowhere.

A God Who Frustrates

1 Cor. 1:18-21, immediately preceding verse 22 quoted above, says, "For the message of the cross is foolishness to those who are perishing, but to us who are being saved it is the power of God. For it is written: 'I will destroy the wisdom of the wise; the intelligence of the intelligent I will frustrate.' Where is the wise man? Where is the scholar? Where is the philosopher of this age? Has not God made foolish the wisdom of the world? For since in the wisdom of God the world through its wisdom did not know him, God was pleased through the foolishness of what was preached to save those who believe."

If the God of the universe has vowed to "destroy the wisdom of the wise" and frustrate "the intelligence of the intelligent" what chance does man have of discovering truth without God? And so the job of deceiving spirits is simply to blind men to that fact while feeding their pride. In that state they are defenseless against many kinds of deception.

With some the devil seeks to discredit the Bible altogether. For example, he encourages those who regard the Bible and belief in God as mere relics of man's supposed primitive past, natural products of the superstitions of a more ignorant age. Deceived by their own prideful intellects, they become fools leading other fools to certain destruction.

Of course another way the devil discredits the Bible in the eyes of many is through false religion. The separation of man from his Creator has left a terrible hole on the inside that makes most men religious in one way or another and so Satan crafts religious substitutes for truth, many full of high-sounding ideas designed to convince thinkers that they have come into possession of truth.

Of course Satan's substitutes for truth share a significant characteristic: they all set forth things that man must DO to fill that hole whereas the gospel of Jesus Christ calls upon man to abandon all trust in his own doing and put all of his trust in what Christ has DONE through the cross. By that measure a lot of religion that claims to be Christian is actually a satanic deception.

"Tolerance"

He also widely promotes a kind of so-called "tolerance" for the many different things people believe. If someone claims to have actual truth — that is, something that is absolutely true — he commits a cardinal sin in the world's eyes! It is not "politically correct" in our day to boldly say of Jesus Christ what Peter said before the religious council in

Acts 4:12 — "Salvation is found in no one else, for there is no other name under heaven given to men by which we must be saved." And add to that Jesus' own words in John 14:6 — "I am the way and the truth and the life. No one comes to the Father except through me."

Satan hates and fears such heaven-inspired clarity and certainty. In fact, he is completely "intolerant" of it! One idea he has widely promoted is the idea that there is no such thing as absolute truth, that each man is entitled to his own "truth." As has often been pointed out, that very idea is absurd and illogical. *The idea itself claims to make an absolute statement about truth!* If there is no absolute truth then how can the idea that there is no absolute truth be true?

Modernism

Of course there are those who — in some sense at least — claim to believe in God and the Bible, yet in reality both are subjected to their own intellects and to "modern" thought. Satan's emissaries accommodate their pride with a wide range of high-sounding ideas that are utterly foreign to genuine truth. Paul referred in part to such things when he warned of "… hollow and deceptive philosophy, which depends on human tradition and the basic principles of this world rather than on Christ." Col. 2:8.

Remember that the basic principles of this world focus on man and his desires here and now and certainly not, "Christ and him crucified." The result is something that falls into the category of what is often called "liberal theology." Any notion that the plain statements of scripture are to be taken at face value is ridiculed.

History is often viewed as "evolutionary" — that is, the human race has evolved from an ignorant primitive state to a state of modern enlightenment. They, of course, are among the enlightened. Thus the real authority is not the inspired Word of God but the ever-evolving ideas of "modern" man.

I remember once hearing a so-called "minister" refer to the words of Jesus about the Holy Spirit guiding us into all truth (John 16:13). That's a wonderful promise but what *he* took that to mean was that truth and our ability to grasp it are evolutionary and change over time. For example, in Bible days homosexuality was regarded as sinful, but now, in a more enlightened age we know that isn't so. God sort of accommodated men's ignorance knowing that in time we would mature as a race and He could broaden our minds.

In other words, the Bible means whatever we want it to mean! Someone has rightly said that the Bible is like a fiddle: you can play any tune you want to on it. Anytime a man puts on the "glasses" of modern worldly philosophy and, trusting in his own intellect, looks into God's Word the devil will twist it into something that doesn't even resemble truth. Make no mistake. There is a demonic inspiration behind the proud intellects of modern man, whether he claims to value the Bible or not. As Paul said in 1 Tim. 4:1, "The Spirit clearly says that in later times some will abandon the faith and follow deceiving spirits and things taught by demons."

The only defense is a humble honest heart that seeks God, knowing that we are helpless apart from His mercy. But where intellectual pride reigns such an approach is held in contempt. That sort of pride is surely a symptom of a "different spirit," one other than Christ, and one that leads its proud and confident victims straight to destruction.

Another side track the devil employs that often leads to a spiritual dead-end is to promote the idea that the key to truth is to delve deeply into the ancient cultures and languages of Bible days. If only we could learn from archaeology, history, and the study of the languages of the Middle East in Bible times then we could unlock the mysteries of the Bible and *really* understand what it teaches!

Some who start down this path are sincere Bible believers but the farther they travel the farther they stray from the simplicity of childlike trust in the Author. It is not that a knowledge of such things cannot have a place but rather that such a pursuit tends to breed a prideful trust in one's own ability to discover truth through the human mind. And, since this kind of pursuit leads away from truth rather than toward it, some even fall away into darkness and unbelief.

Private Interpreters

One tactic the devil employs, often with sincere and zealous people who hold a strong view of the Bible as God's word, is to provoke them to become "private interpreters." Peter encouraged his readers to pay close attention to the word of the prophets. Then he added these words: "Above all, you must understand that no prophecy of Scripture came about by the prophet's own interpretation. For prophecy never had its origin in the will of man, but men spoke from God as they were carried along by the Holy Spirit." 2 Peter 1:20-21. Above all! Something we **must** understand.

First of all we see that the prophets themselves operated under divine inspiration. They didn't give out *their* opinions or *their* interpretations but God's message. Prophecy was serious business. Moses' law prescribed the death penalty for false prophets! Deut. 13:1-5.

But the fact is that we need the same divine inspiration, the same divine overshadowing to *understand* the scriptures. Everything about God's kingdom is supernatural and requires God's active participation. I have a friend who is fond of saying, "The Bible is one book that cannot be understood without the Author." That is true. But the devil promotes an insidious lie: **His lie is that the Bible can be understood by the human mind through diligent study**.

On the surface that idea sounds very reasonable. After all, the Bible was written for human beings to read. Wouldn't it make sense that it was meant to be understood? And doesn't Paul say in 2 Tim. 2:15, "Study to shew thyself approved unto God, a workman that needeth not to be ashamed, rightly dividing the word of truth"? KJV.

The misuse of that verse is responsible for a lot of error and deception in Christendom. People read the word "study" in the King James Version and substitute a modern meaning for the word, for example, as in the "study" of mathematics or science. In that sense "studying" does indeed mean employing the power of one's mind to understand some aspect of human knowledge.

But the sense of Paul's instruction to Timothy was to be "diligent," to "do your best to present yourself to God as one approved." NASB, NIV. It is not about a *method* but about *faithfulness and effort*. That effort was to be directed towards "correctly" or "accurately" handling the word of truth. The context deals with the problem of false teaching and quarreling about words.

But can that be done with mere intellect? In Matt.11:25 Jesus said, "I praise you, Father, Lord of heaven and earth, because you have hidden these things from the wise and learned, and revealed them to little children." In the context he was talking about the inability of the people of that generation to understand the things of God. No matter what he did or said they considered him wrong and "out-of-step."

But the fact is that *they* were the ones who were out-of-step — with God! They were blind and didn't know it. We have an expression in our day: "often wrong; never in doubt." In this case they were always wrong. Being confident you are right when you are wrong is a bad place to be.

No one was more diligent in studying scripture than were the scribes and Pharisees. In John 5:39-40 Jesus said of them, "You diligently study the Scriptures because you think that by them you possess eternal life. These are the Scriptures that testify about me, yet you refuse to come to me to have life." They were fond of examining every little detail of their scriptures, putting each one under a "theological microscope," debating its meaning and implications, but despite all their diligent study they were blind and deaf to the divine Author and His Son.

The result was a religion built upon the interpretations and traditions of men. Jesus quoted from Isaiah — one of their revered prophets — to set their religion in its true light: "These people honor me with their lips, but their hearts are far from me. They worship me in vain; their teachings are but rules taught by men." Matt. 15:8-9.

If the key to spiritual knowledge is mere study of the scriptures then why didn't Paul say that the gospel he preached was the result of diligent study on his part? Why did he rather say, "I received it by revelation from Jesus Christ"? Gal. 1:12. And Paul had come from that very tradition of "study" and "debate." I'm afraid that tradition is alive and well in our day.

Modern religion is full of "private interpreters" of scripture. Actually, the idea that scripture is something that needs to be "interpreted" is — at best — misleading. It suggests that God has simply given us a book and left us to figure it out as best we can! The result of that kind of thinking is that each one feels he has the right and ability to apply his mind to the Bible and come up with his own interpretation. And the result of all that private interpreting is the Babylon of religious confusion we observe in our world — and Satan loves it.

The internet provides an amazing means of communication — of all kinds. One kind that is pertinent to our subject has to do with religious debate. Many are the websites that host online discussions of various theological questions, and vigorous debates pop up in many other places as well.

Just the thought of wading through most of that kind of thing makes me ill! Each one argues that his interpretation is the right one and the other person's is wrong. Sometimes the debating becomes downright ugly. Some are contending for a particular theological or religious tradition they happen to favor and others are true private interpreters trying to add their own novel slant to the discussion.

Not only is it not edifying most of the time, it is downright depressing. The sense I get is that a bunch of religious people, operating completely in the natural realm, are fighting about things none of them understands. It is the spirit of it that so often gives it away. Nothing is accomplished but strife and confusion.

Some websites are devoted to a particular point of view and therefore many like-minded people "hang out" there. But woe to any "troll" who happens to chime in with a contrary opinion! They will quickly gang up on him, typically with little or no grace, all the while congratulating each other in how "sound in the faith" they are.

Single Issue Captives

Over the years I've had all sorts of people write and email me trying to convince me of some doctrine or idea. It's one thing to humbly consider honest questions but I'm talking about the kind of person who has latched onto some particular idea and who has set out on a mission to convince everyone they can. Sometimes there is almost an air of desperation as in, "I have THE key to what's wrong with the modern church. If only people would listen!"

There's an inspiration behind that sort thing — and it's not good. Do you detect the spirit of religion in it? It's like God has given us laws to obey in order to win acceptance and blessing and there's something we're not "doing right" (observing Christmas, worshipping on the wrong day, using the wrong divine name, etc., etc.) and so He's standing back waiting for us to practice the religion He has instituted correctly. There is indeed a lot wrong with the modern church: Jesus is outside knocking, asking to be let in! Rev. 3:20.

I remember one man who emailed me several times contending for a particular "out-of-the-mainstream" theological point of view. I tried at first to honestly and gently consider and answer his questions and points but it became obvious — and he even said as much — that he was just looking for a "sparring partner" to exercise his debating skills! No heart for truth. If I didn't happen to comment on a particular point he attempted to make he presumed that I agreed with him! As it became obvious what was happening I gently pointed him to the phrase from 2 Tim. 2:14 (KJV) which speaks of striving about words to no profit and so our "discussions" ended.

It is even possible to contend for something that is actually true, yet do it apart from God's Spirit and it actually does harm instead of good. We don't just need truth; we need the SPIRIT of truth as well. Dead truth kills spiritually. 2 Cor. 3:6.

Paul's Warnings

In Paul's day the "scriptures" consisted of the Old Testament and many people were going around as supposed teachers of those scriptures. Listen to some of the things Paul said about them, and as you do, relate what he says to the world of today.

1 Tim. 1:3-7 — "As I urged you when I went into Macedonia, stay there in Ephesus so that you may command certain men not to teach false doctrines any longer nor to devote themselves to myths and endless genealogies. These promote controversies rather than God's work — which is by faith. The goal of this command is love, which comes from a pure heart and a good conscience and a sincere faith. Some have wandered away from these and turned to meaningless talk. They want to be teachers of the law, but they do not know what they are talking about or what they so confidently affirm."

1 Tim. 6:3-5 — "If anyone teaches false doctrines and does not agree to the sound instruction of our Lord Jesus Christ and to godly teaching, he is conceited and understands nothing. He has an unhealthy interest in controversies and quarrels about words that result in envy, strife, malicious talk, evil suspicions and constant friction between men of corrupt mind, who have been robbed of the truth and who think that godliness is a means to financial gain." (That last part certainly fits in many places today!)

2 Tim. 2:14 — "Keep reminding them of these things. Warn them before God against quarreling about words; it is of no value, and only ruins those who listen." NIV.

2 Tim. 2:23-26 — "Don't have anything to do with foolish and stupid arguments, because you know they produce quarrels. And the Lord's servant must not quarrel; instead, he must be kind to everyone, able to teach, not resentful. Those who oppose him he must gently instruct, in the hope that God will grant them repentance leading them to a knowledge of the truth, and that they will come to their senses and escape from the trap of the devil, who has taken them captive to do his will." Notice the involvement of the devil in all this.

Titus 3:9 — "But avoid foolish controversies and genealogies and arguments and quarrels about the law, because these are unprofitable and useless."

Peter's reference to Paul is interesting in 2 Peter 3:15-16 — "Bear in mind that our Lord's patience means salvation, just as our dear brother Paul also wrote you with the wisdom that God gave him. He writes the same way in all his letters, speaking in them of these matters. His letters contain some things that are hard to understand, which ignorant and unstable people distort, as they do the other Scriptures, to their own destruction."

In Luke 24 we find two of Jesus' followers walking from Jerusalem to Emmaus, a village about 7 miles away. As they walked they talked together, struggling to understand recent events, the crucifixion of Jesus and the reports of some of the women that he had appeared to them alive. As they walked along they were joined by Jesus himself, yet they were unable at the time to recognize him.

They recounted what they had been discussing and then Jesus said, "How foolish you are, and how slow of heart to believe all that the prophets have spoken! Did not the Christ have to suffer these things and then enter his glory?" Then the account says, "And beginning with Moses and all the Prophets, he explained to them what was said in all the Scriptures concerning himself." Luke 24:25-27.

Think about it! Not only did the most brilliant and diligent religious scholars of the day not understand their own scriptures, Jesus' own followers were clueless as to their meaning — until he specifically opened their understanding. What a deception it is to suppose that anyone can grasp truth apart from him who IS truth!

In 1 Cor. 8:1-2 Paul said, "Knowledge puffs up, but love builds up. The man who thinks he knows something does not yet know as he ought to know." We would all do well to maintain some humility about all the things we think we know. In 1 Cor. 13:9 even Paul said, "For we know in part and we prophesy in part ...."

We Need God

The reality is that genuine knowledge of spiritual things comes ONLY by divine revelation (or illumination, if you prefer). A man can put a scripture under a "microscope," turn it every way but loose, and still know nothing of any spiritual value. We need God! Many of those who "study" the scriptures will give lip service to the idea that they need God to open our understanding, yet in practice they rely on their own intellects to reason out answers they seek, or worse, to "cherry pick" proof texts to prop up their pet ideas.

We need a spirit of humility and childlikeness, one that genuinely TRUSTS God. We need to be willing to honestly say we don't know something if we don't. We need the attitude, "Lord, you know and I don't. Furthermore, I *can't* know unless you show me. And if in your wisdom you don't show me a particular thing, that's OK. I trust your wisdom and rest in your love. I'm depending upon You alone to show me what I need to know when I need to know it, and to give me the grace to walk in it."

And even where we think we know a thing we need to leave room for greater light that refines, and even corrects. We need to be willing not to insist on prying into something God isn't revealing just to satisfy curiosity, ours or someone else's. I readily confess that I have not always walked as well as I should have in these principles but the farther I go the more I realize how little I really know, and how dependent I am upon God.

The Spirit of truth will never leave the scriptures behind, but will rather shine a clearer and clearer light upon them as the age draws to a close. He will make truth known to those who humbly and honestly seek God from their hearts.

The spirit of error will seek to divorce the scriptures from their Author in one way or another, promoting such things as pride, tradition, strife, debate, confusion, and anything else that conforms to the wisdom of this present world.

The "Greek" is an unbeliever because he elevates his own intellect above faith. He trusts in it as a reliable guide in his search for truth. He requires God to bow down to his intellect by providing answers that he approves of before he will consider believing. He will not take the place of a humble child before the all-knowing Sovereign of the universe, seeking and trusting Him because of who He is even when there are things he cannot understand.

And behind that "Greek" there are wicked spirits at work whose job it is to keep him from genuine truth by any means possible.

Chapter 8

Signs and Wonders

Christ dwells in his body, the church, by the Spirit and is literally her life. Apart from his abiding presence so-called churches are nothing but expressions of lifeless religion, counterfeits populated by all manner of religious demons who seek to blind people to the living Christ. These demons do whatever it takes to convince their victims that their religious counterfeits are actually of God.

The greatest stronghold that the devil has is not over a man who lives in open wickedness but rather over a man who has embraced a lie, yet who believes he has come into possession of truth. He feels no need. There is no blindness like religious blindness since that condition promotes the illusion that its victims not only can see, but that they are among the enlightened. John 9:39-41.

Religious spirits deal with all kinds of people in their efforts to deceive and so their tactics necessarily vary according to their targets. We have referred to two broad categories of people, typified by the Jews and Greeks of Paul's day. 1 Cor. 1:22-24 says, "Jews demand miraculous signs and Greeks look for wisdom, but we preach Christ crucified: a stumbling block to Jews and foolishness to Gentiles, but to those whom God has called, both Jews and Greeks, Christ the power of God and the wisdom of God."

We have discussed the "Greek" type, those who rely on their intellects, and noted a few of the symptoms of the workings of spirits on such people. But many others are like the "Jews" in their emphasis upon the miraculous. They insist that God prove Himself by doing something they can detect with their earthly senses. This presents a wide range of opportunities for deception by the kingdom of darkness.

Light and darkness: that is the battle. 1 John 1:5 reminds us, "This is the message we have heard from him and declare to you: God is light; in him there is no darkness at all." His very being enlightens, imparting knowledge, wisdom, and understanding. Darkness, on the other hand, is not merely the absence of light but a very real evil force that imprisons men's minds, suppressing light and blinding them to it. Col. 1:13, John 1:5, Acts 26:18, 1 John 2:11, Matt. 6:23, John 12:35-40.

The demand for the miraculous itself takes two broad forms. In some, the "demand" is not sincere but is actually a defense *against* God and light. They don't really want light and are looking for an excuse to reject Him. Others, blind to true divinely-enabled faith, demand instead that God meet them on *their* terms, as we have said, by proving Himself in some way that can be detected through earthly senses. They seek signs for reasons other than to fulfill God's will and purpose.

A Wicked and Adulterous Generation

Many of the Jews of Jesus' day were examples of the first type. Of them Jesus said, "A wicked and adulterous generation asks for a miraculous sign!" Matt. 12:39. Their true nature was described by Jesus' words in John 3:19-20 — "This is the verdict: Light has come into the world, but men loved darkness instead of light because their deeds were evil. Everyone who does evil hates the light, and will not come into the light for fear that his deeds will be exposed."

God does indeed sometimes perform miraculous deeds in bearing witness to the gospel but it takes a lot more than a miracle to bring men to true faith. Many suppose that if only men could see God's power in action in some way they would believe. Not so.

Think of all the wonders the Israelites saw in coming out of Egypt. Yet God rejected most of a whole generation. Of them He said, "Their hearts are always going astray, and they have not known my ways." Heb. 3:10. Another spirit held them in a prison house of darkness and unbelief. Their problem was not ignorance, but rebellion.

Some people who see signs and wonders might become religious out of fear but only those in whose hearts God's Spirit has been at work will truly believe. Minds and emotions may sometimes be stirred but it is the heart that reflects our true condition. Proverbs 4:23.

Consider the story of the rich man and Lazarus in Luke 16:19-31. Each one dies, the rich man finding himself in torment, and Lazarus, a beggar on earth, finding a place of rest at "Abraham's side." At first the rich man begs Abraham for help — even a little bit of water to cool his parched tongue, but finding this impossible, he begs that his still-living brothers be warned.

"Abraham replied, 'They have Moses and the Prophets; let them listen to them.'" Verse 29.

The man continued, "'No, father Abraham,' he said, 'but if someone from the dead goes to them, they will repent.'"

Abraham's response: "If they do not listen to Moses and the Prophets, they will not be convinced even if someone rises from the dead."

No sign would ever have been enough despite the demands of religious leaders for one. The truth is that they had many signs all around them of God's power at work in His Son but they were blind. Like darkness, unbelief is an evil, demonic force that possesses men's hearts and minds. It causes them — as Jesus said — to "love darkness rather than light."

Why? What would cause a man to do such a thing? *Their deeds are evil*. Note that darkness is not even something they see as evil; **they love it!** As Isaiah prophesied: "Woe to those who call evil good and good evil…." Isaiah 5:20.

They are prisoners of sin with no desire to change. Thus any demand for a sign springs not from a desire to be convinced and believe but from a desire for an excuse to continue as they are. Jesus recognized their condition and responded accordingly. *No one has ever been lost for lack of a sign.*

Sign-Seekers

But others can readily be described as "sign-seekers." They want something to believe in but need something they consider to be evidence. We live in a sense-governed world: what we can see, hear, feel, taste, and smell. Many religious people are sign-seekers in that they want a God whose presence and activity they can detect with their natural senses. What they call "faith" is entirely dependent upon those senses. God and His presence are equated with such things as supernatural manifestations, strong emotions and even physical sensations.

This makes them very vulnerable to spirits who certainly have power to affect our senses. Jesus warned of this in Matt. 24:24 — "For false christs and false prophets will appear and perform great signs and miracles to deceive even the elect — if that were possible." (Thank God for that last part!) Paul referred to the same thing in 2 Thess. 2:9-10 where he spoke of the "work of Satan displayed in all kinds of counterfeit miracles, signs and wonders, and in every sort of evil that deceives those who are perishing."

People love miracles. Great crowds often followed Jesus, not because they were drawn to the message of salvation but because they were amazed at the miracles he performed. For example, John 6:1-2 says, "Some time after this, Jesus crossed to the far shore of the Sea of Galilee (that is, the Sea of Tiberias), and a great crowd of people followed him because they saw the miraculous signs he had performed on the sick."

In this passage we find Jesus multiplying loaves and fishes to feed this great crowd. What was their response? Was it to repent of their sins and seek for eternal life? No! They wanted to take Jesus by force and make him king! With such a king they would never lack anything. How obvious is it that their motive was entirely earthly and selfish. They were blind as to who Jesus was and why he had come.

And it wasn't long before the great crowds left when Jesus gave them, not miracles, but uncomfortable truth. John 6:60-66. Nothing will cause a sign-seeker to go his way like uncompromising gospel truth that shines a light on his heart's need and seeks to bring about true repentance. He will run in search of the latest sign, miracle, or experience and believe himself to be spiritually superior for having done so.

What is it about signs, wonders, and spiritual experiences that people find so appealing? What are they seeking? Remember the description of what motivates people of the world in 1 John 2:16 — "the cravings of sinful man, the lust of his eyes and the boasting of what he has and does." Such desires often seek their fulfillment in the realm of the miraculous.

Unquestionably the motivation in some is that people find such things entertaining. People love excitement, the "wow" factor. Where some are thrilled at musical or athletic performances, others are like those who followed Jesus. They want to be amazed and excited, and the idea that God is involved in some way is really a bonus. It makes their pursuit of supernatural entertainment seem OK and they bask in the atmosphere, expecting that God is pleased with their interest in "spiritual" things.

But the truth is that they are no more interested in the things of God than were those who stopped following Jesus that day. A God who entertains me with miracles — great! But a God who tells me truth I don't want to hear — that's another story. That can't be God!

Such a view of God leaves one wide open to deception. Miracles become proof-positive of God's presence and activity. A symptom of deception in this area is when there is an undue emphasis upon the miraculous. That kind of emphasis will surely draw a crowd — but to what? Is God's priority to amaze people with miracles or to rescue lost helpless sinners through the gospel? Is His emphasis upon "power" or upon Christ and him crucified?

Many religious gatherings that emphasize miracles are essentially shows. The religious practitioner — often a healer — is the showman who hopes to amaze his followers with his ability to use "God's power." He basks in fame and fortune at the expense of those followers and justifies it all as "the work of God." Yet how many like him will be among those to whom Jesus will one day say, "I never knew you. Away from me, you evildoers!" Matt. 7:21-23. Some of them will claim to have cast out demons and performed many miracles!

Can you imagine Jesus putting on a show as so many do in our day? He helped people in real need, motivated by compassion, led by God, often privately, never majoring on the miracles. Drama and showmanship played no part. He didn't need someone playing an organ to set the mood! His focus was always on imparting truth that would set his hearers free. John 8:31-32. He never sought to glorify himself but only the Father who had sent him. John 7:18. He only did what the Father showed him to do. John 5:19.

Glory Seekers

Of course, the same miracle power that entertains and amazes some begets in others an ambition to **be** miracle workers themselves. They follow, but motivated by a desire to learn the secret, to acquire the power to perform their own miracles. Despite their attempts to pass off their ambition as "spiritual," it is typically nothing but pride and a desire to win the adulation of the crowds.

A scriptural example can be found in Acts 8 where we read about Philip carrying the gospel to Samaria. There was a man who lived there who had some kind of occult power by which he amazed the Samaritans and gained a reputation as "the Great Power." Acts 8:9-11.

God used Philip to perform many genuine miracles — in order to bear witness to the gospel — and these miracles were such that even Simon was amazed and "believed." After he and many others were baptized in water Peter and John were sent from Jerusalem and laid hands on the believers that they might receive the Holy Spirit.

As Simon observed this his true motivation was revealed. In verses 18 and 19 we see him offer the apostles money that he might likewise have the ability to impart the Holy Spirit.

"Peter answered: 'May your money perish with you, because you thought you could buy the gift of God with money! You have no part or share in this ministry, because your heart is not right before God. Repent of this wickedness and pray to the Lord. Perhaps he will forgive you for having such a thought in your heart. For I see that you are full of bitterness and captive to sin.'" Acts 8:20-23. History seems to suggest that Simon never did repent or escape his addiction to pride and glory-seeking. He died an enemy to Christ and the gospel.

We children of Adam are proud creatures. At best pride is a problem even when God's power is truly at work. Look what became necessary in 2 Cor. 12:7-10 to keep Paul humble. But when religious people pursue miracle power outside of the will and purpose of God there is nothing left but the working of demons. Any glorying will be in miracles and men, not in Christ and the cross.

Blessing Seekers

On one level miracles are very entertaining but on another we by nature love the idea of power that triumphs over the trials and difficulties of earthly life. No matter how hard we may try it is evident that we human beings are not in control. Life is full of uncertainty. Things happen that we don't anticipate and for which we are unprepared. A man may become rich only to find out he has cancer. Someone unexpectedly dies. The idea of gaining access to supernatural power in these things is very appealing. This is what draws some to witchcraft.

Those fed miraculously by Jesus saw him as one who had such power and they desired it that they might meet life's challenges. As we have said, their interest was not spiritual at all. Most people who flocked to Jesus simply wanted their problems fixed. And so, people chase signs and wonders, not only seeking entertainment or prideful recognition, but also power over earthly trials, whether related to health, prosperity, or other circumstances.

When you consider the matter honestly what many really seek is to make God their servant, a sort of heavenly "Mr. Fix-it." They are looking for the secrets involved in "getting God to do what I want." The idea that God has His own plan and purpose never enters their minds. They constantly seek the latest "formula," or the "magic prayer." If they hear of someone who seems to have some success in making things happen they run after them in hopes of learning the secret.

Witchcraft and Magic

This pursuit has far more in common with witchcraft and magic than most would like to admit. I have no doubt that many would highly resent this suggestion but it is true. The essence of man's fall into sin is that he seeks to be in control, to assert his own will, to be his own god.

It probably sounds like a contradiction to say that trying to get God to do something for me can be seeking to be my own god but it is true. The real question is: whose will is paramount? Is it really God's will and purpose we seek, or our own? Is He our servant, some magic genie who exists to do our bidding?

Those who practice witchcraft or magic usually do so as part of an elaborate belief system. They may see magical powers as simply part of the natural order of things, just as physical laws are. Or, they may believe in their own essential divinity and seek to tap into that. And, of course, some consciously seek to invoke the intervention of demons and heathen "gods."

Regardless of the particular belief system some of the basic characteristics involved are ritual, incantation, and "faith." These are seen as the means by which one is able to invoke or tap into supernatural power to achieve a certain result.

Rituals are simply carefully prescribed things to do. They could involve most anything. The key is to do the ritual correctly. Rituals involve such things as particular places, times, objects, and actions. Go to a special mountain or temple during the full moon; bring certain objects with you and arrange them a certain way, etc., etc. The key is that whatever the ritual involves, it is something the person or persons must DO.

Incantations are simply the precise words that must be said in connection with rituals. Once again, notice who is in charge! It is as though the power is just there waiting to be tapped if only one DOES and SAYS the right things. Magic is very formulaic. Employing the correct formula is just about everything.

The other ingredient is that one must believe in what one is doing. It is not enough to do everything mechanically. It is important that heart and mind be engaged. It is not hard to see these principles as powerful tools used by demon spirits to enslave people in darkness. Such simple things as Ouija boards have been used by demons to gain a stronghold. People may think they are just "playing," but the devil isn't.

As I observe the professing church world of today it seems to me that there is a lot of "magic" in the approach of many to the things of God. Some of this can even creep into the thinking of real believers but it is very evident in the many who are simply religious.

God surely does supernaturally intervene in the affairs of men — according to His own purposes. The Word of God gives us many examples of this. Such examples together with the many precious promises God has given us are meant to encourage us to seek Him and look to Him in every situation. But the key — again — is *His* purposes and not ours.

A Divine Vending Machine

However, it is an unfortunate tendency in man's corrupted thinking to pervert the rich provisions of God's grace into a resource for selfish, earthly purposes. It is almost as though God has provided us with a great heavenly "vending machine" and the Bible is a book of magic that shows us how to extract its blessings. Just put your "money" in the slot, press the right button and out pops the blessing!

There is in the minds of many a very simplistic view of life: God always wants people to be happy, healthy, and prosperous; the key to enjoying these things is our faith; if something bad happens in our lives it is caused by the devil and we have the right to make it "go away."

A lot of people have been brought into great bondage through such teaching. Essentially, if they are not happy, healthy, and prosperous it is *their* fault for not having enough faith. And so they struggle along, *trying* to muster up faith, often attending emotionally-charged gatherings as though that would somehow help them to reach the right button on the vending machine, and often discouraged and condemned in their own minds that what they seek seems to remain out of reach.

And if someone they know about seems to be successful in their pursuit of blessings it becomes a "sign" that they are on the right track, both encouraging them that blessings are available and yet simultaneously discouraging them by reminding them of their own failure to obtain them.

On the other hand, if they *do* seemingly obtain a divine blessing then then there is the very human tendency to glory in the blessing and in the faith that obtained it. Their experience becomes yet another sign that is used to encourage other sign-seekers and to validate their own efforts.

What I have described happens in far too many places. It is like a religious "treadmill" on which people are encouraged to run faster, to try harder, yet no matter how fast they run or how hard they try they go nowhere. All they get for their efforts is tired and discouraged. Of course the devil knows just when and how to inject a note of encouragement and vain hope through someone's experience.

What? Why? How?

Questions that need to be considered are these: *What* are you seeking? *Why* are you seeking it? *How* are you seeking it? Is it about God's will or yours? Is it about eternal purposes or temporal earthly blessings? Is it about God's glory or yours?

God is mindful of our earthly needs. We are encouraged by these words in Matt. 6:33 to "... seek first his kingdom and his righteousness, and all these things will be given to you as well." What things? Earthly necessities. The same passage warns in verse 24 that it is impossible to serve two masters. We cannot serve both God and money. Verse 21 reminds us that, "... where your treasure is, there will your heart be also."

Does any of this mean that it's not right or "spiritual" to seek God about earthly needs and trials? Of course not! We are told to "Cast all your anxiety on him because he cares for you." 1 Peter 5:7. He wants us to bring every care to Him — but with an understanding heart and a submissive spirit.

He is focused on eternity while we tend to be focused on earthly things. We seek comfort, ease, and prosperity; He seeks Christlikeness and that His name might be glorified. Each person, each circumstance is unique and He has a purpose in it. Sometimes He indeed does something obviously supernatural and wonderful. Other times His plan involves such things as pain and suffering as well as other trials and difficulties.

Paul's experience in 2 Cor. 12:1-10 is a perfect illustration. The great revelations given to Paul had left him vulnerable to a common human weakness: pride. To counter that the Lord allowed a demon to harass Paul. Surely Paul knew all the formulas and proof-texts for making devils go away but this time they didn't work.

So he prayed. And he prayed. And he prayed. Did he do wrong in this? Of course not. But notice that he didn't "claim" victory or assert his own will and "faith" in some way. He just persistently brought the need to God. Finally God answered him, but not by making the devil leave! He helped Paul to see the reason and so Paul humbled himself and grew spiritually.

His experience has been an encouragement to countless believers ever since. In some situations it is not God's will to make the difficulty "go away," rather, He gives grace to endure. Paul wanted to serve God effectively and initially thought that the harrassing demon was an obstacle. He came to see that the real obstacle to effective service was his own self and pride and that battling that demon in God's strength kept self and pride in check.

Did he grumble about all this? No! Once he understood, he *gloried* in his own weakness and dependence upon the grace of God because through that Christ's power rested upon him making his ministry truly effective.

A Way Out

A favorite scripture for a believer to quote in a time of trial is found in 1 Cor. 10:13 where we read, "No temptation has seized you except what is common to man. And God is faithful; he will not let you be tempted beyond what you can bear. But when you are tempted, he will also provide a way out so that you can stand up under it."

It is easy to focus on the words, "a way out" and miss the "so that you can stand up under it" part. God can make trials and difficulties disappear — if that is His purpose. However, much of the time, His purpose is fulfilled when we depend upon His strength to *endure* the trial.

Healing

One area of controversy and misunderstanding concerns healing. Everyone agrees that God can and does heal. But some teach that it is *always* His will to heal. This teaching effectively turns health and illness into signs! They become signs of faith or the lack thereof and this tends to divide people into two spiritual categories. Those who enjoy good health are in the superior category of those who have faith and those who are sick have a measure of condemnation added to their sickness due to their perceived lack of faith.

Such teaching has much bad fruit but one thing that comes to mind is that there is a great deal of focus on physical healing — and not so much on the things that really matter to God. Ok, so I'm sick. What do I need to do to get well? More faith? How do I get that? Maybe I need to run to the healing crusade and get so-and-so to lay hands on me. Ok, that didn't work. What next? And on and on it goes with life becoming all about ME and getting well physically.

Just about anyone who struggles with ill health and seeks to serve God has experienced some of these things. They are natural to us. But I thank God for the many testimonies I've heard over the years of some who have been brought into a deep and wonderful relationship with God *through* their infirmity — and never been healed this side of eternity!

What believer has ever read the writings of Amy Carmichael and not been blessed and encouraged in their faith? Yet her writings came out of deep suffering as she was a bed-ridden invalid who experienced a lot of pain over many years. Do you think she is looking down from heaven and complaining that it wasn't worth it and that God did wrong by not healing her? I don't think so! Do you really think Jesus met her at heaven's gate and said, "I'm glad to see you but you should have had more faith"?

A more current example is Joni Eareckson Tada who suffered a terrible diving accident at 17 in which she was permanently paralyzed. She went through some very deep spiritual waters coming to terms with her accident but her testimony today is that God has brought her into a deep and precious relationship with God through it all — so wonderful that if she could trade it all for perfect health she wouldn't. In addition she has been given a ministry and a testimony that has reached around the world and brought much glory to God. She longs for heaven not so much that she might walk again but that she might see her Saviour face to face! Walking will be a bonus!

One way the Bible is sometimes used almost like a book of spells concerns drawing a formula for all time out of an experience recorded there. The underlying idea is that by doing a particular thing, God was revealing THE WAY He works, a pattern that can be repeated anytime by one who has the needed faith. It is one thing if God leads and imparts faith but apart from that we're back to the "vending machine" approach to God.

One example that comes to mind concerns a certain prayer recorded in an obscure passage in the Old Testament that was widely promoted as "a prayer that God always answers." That is quite a leap of logic and basically turns a prayer almost into a magic incantation. Building a doctrine based on an experience is not a good idea.

Tongues

Another example of an experience turned into a doctrine concerns Pentecost. On that occasion God did a wonderful and special thing to bear witness to Christ's exaltation and the gospel. (By the way, just to show the power of tradition: they were in the temple, NOT in the upper room! They may have stayed in the upper room by night but they spent most of their "waiting for the promised Holy Spirit" time in the temple. Read Luke 24:53.)

As the disciples were there in the temple among the throngs gathered for the Jewish feast of Pentecost the Holy Spirit came upon them. There were individual tongues of fire that rested upon them and they were given the power to testify to the wonderful works of God in the languages of those present — a special miracle for the occasion.

There were a few other times when people were recorded as having spoken in tongues but in each case there was a particular reason. The Samaritans represented a departure from "Jews-only." The household of Cornelius even more so. God bore a special witness to these unfolding stages in the outreach of His kingdom.

The Ephesian disciples in Acts 20 had been ministered an incomplete faith (the baptism of John) and God gave them a special manifestation of His Spirit that demonstrated the difference. Even then some apparently prophesied rather than speaking in tongues.

Speaking in tongues has become for many a major "sign" that believers are taught to seek (or least, go by). But when Peter was explaining his going to the household of Cornelius to share the gospel he said, "As I began to speak, the Holy Spirit came on them as he had come on us at the beginning." Acts 11:15. Why did Peter refer all the way back to "the beginning" if this experience happened regularly?

God can and does express Himself in many ways during experiences but so many have turned what happened at Pentecost into a specific pattern meant to apply to all believers since. That absolutely turns people into sign-seekers. As in the case of healing it produces the "haves" — who often feel superior — and the "have nots" who feel "less than" and condemned.

Awhile back a brother and I happened to attend a Pentecost celebration, a gathering of churches who believed that doctrine. One of the major objectives of the meeting, it quickly became apparent, was to get anyone who had not had that particular experience to enter into it. It was very apparent to me and several others that they were striving in themselves — striving to replicate the experience of Pentecost. If only they had managed to get those who came to the "altar" to utter a few nonsensical syllables they would have taken that as a sure sign that the meeting had been a great success.

Now I'm sure that there were some there who genuinely loved the Lord but that doctrine had become a spiritual sidetrack. Of course it would be equally wrong to say that God *never* does anything like that, that the gift of tongues, prophesying, and the like have all passed away. That's not right either. The truth is that we need God, however He chooses to work.

But relying on a sign like speaking in tongues has surely given the devil a lot to work with. When people crave a particular sign more than they do the Lord Himself, they are liable to get one, but it won't be from the Lord.

I remember a time in my own experience when the Lord dealt with me in this area. I was among those who spent a lot of time preaching about this other spiritual realm that God wanted us to enter. This was preached as something apart from "getting saved." Tongues or no tongues I wanted to enter in but although people around me seemingly did, I sort of "hit a wall" one weekend and got mad at God for a few days! Why was He leaving me out?

About midweek, after I had pouted for several emotionally-flat days, I quietly came to a point of surrender in which I essentially told the Lord, "I'll serve you even if I never have a feeling." There was no wave of emotion, no great breakthrough — but way down deep — in my spirit — there was a measure of peace that let me know that the Lord was listening. I hadn't been held by the strength of some experience but by something much deeper. Even without any emotions whatsoever I *knew* God was real and that there was no real choice but to trust Him. He graciously and lovingly waited me out!

The Christian life is a life of faith. It doesn't depend upon what we see or feel in the sense realm. Many times we are called to walk through dry places in the spirit and stand fast in our faith nonetheless. But many people depend heavily upon their feelings or upon some experience they had once yet seemingly have little or no genuine faith. They are sign-seekers. God seeks those who want Him and trust His word with no conditions. A believer does not say, "I'll believe you IF...." He simply believes, not just a bunch of religious doctrines and principles but in the PERSON of God. It is a heart of trust thing and not a sign thing.

Many other examples could be cited that would illustrate what Jesus meant when he warned of lying signs and wonders. Suppose you wanted to go to New York and you came to a sign that said, "Welcome to New York" — BUT you were actually entering Chicago! That would be a lying sign.

The sign itself would be real but the MESSAGE conveyed by the sign would be a lie. That is what so often happens in spiritual matters. Many outward things are taken as proof-positive signs of God's favor and Christ's presence. Just a few examples will illustrate the principle.

Emotions

Whenever God has truly visited people with His manifest presence, people's emotions have been deeply touched. His presence brings repentance and brokenness followed by worship that flows from the depths of one's soul, all reflected in the emotions of those present.

However, just because God's presence touches people emotionally, it does not follow that a religious gathering attended by great emotion is necessarily evidence of God's presence! "Come to such-and-such a place where thousands will gather to worship God and have a blast" is something that can be produced on a purely human level. We are emotional beings and there are many things that can stir those emotions. But what is the "engine" behind them? When God is truly present, people are confronted at the heart level and either transformed — or they run! An expression of religiously-generated emotion is no substitute.

Loud, energetic, and sometimes emotional music, stirring speakers, the presence of large numbers of like-minded people, can produce a rich emotional experience for those in attendance. Such gatherings are very much part of our culture and not necessarily connected with God at all. We see them in the realm of business, politics, entertainment, social action groups, motivational meetings. I remember years ago being in Amway rallies that featured all of those things.

Religion has widely adopted these forms and often glories in large impressive gatherings where religious emotions are stirred, people are "excited," and thousands worship God with uplifted hands. I don't doubt that some of them do! Thank God! But there is far more "religious production" than divine presence in much of that.

What would happen if Jesus were to step onto the platform, silence the ear-deafening, flesh-arousing music, and, with genuine divine anointing, address the true heart needs of those present. How many of those present would say, "Yes! This is what I have been waiting for!"? I fear that most would wish he would simply go away and let them get back to their "blast." They didn't come for *that*, they came for a good time!

The Jews of Jesus' day had their religious forms too, but when he brought the light of God's presence and truth into their gatherings they were ready to kill him — and ultimately did. Never forget that religious form — any religious form — begets *hatred for God* and resists His presence. 2 Timothy 3:5. Of course that hatred is not apparent unless God actually shows up!

Where God is truly present and working there will surely be emotion, but self and sin will be seen in the light of that presence, heartfelt repentance and brokenness will result, and joyful worship and praise will flow out of that. You won't need a deafening sound system! A humanly-engineered religious experience, no matter how sincerely done, is no substitute. Nor is deep emotion proof that God is present.

Revival

One particular area that typically involves emotion is that of "revival." There are many accounts of both past and present movings of God in the earth attended by deep emotional responses. That understandably begets in some a hunger to see God move in revival power again. That is a wonderful desire — so long as we realize that it can't be engineered by us nor do we have the right to dictate to God how or when He is to move!

One weakness that I have observed — and experienced! — is that those who hunger for "revival" are often the very ones most in need of it! They imagine that the hunger itself sets them spiritually above others and drives them to pray for those less spiritual than themselves that God would revive "them." True revival never breaks out until those who seek it first experience their own genuine repentance, humility, and brokenness before God.

Two experiences come to mind. When I was in college I twice traveled with a gospel quartet for summer ministry. One of our stops was a Bible Conference at a campground. The special speaker for the conference had a particular emphasis in his ministry on "revival." He spent his time recounting tales of how had God moved in the past, particularly in the famous Welsh Revival of the early 1900s.

As many have pointed out, that revival was preceded by a great deal of prayer by a group of ordinary men who devoted themselves to hours of earnest prayer daily over a long time. And so one thing the speaker did was to organize round-the-clock prayer for revival. Surely there is nothing wrong with encouraging people to seek God but it became sadly apparent that his effort was largely a human one, striving to replicate what happened in Wales, as though it could be engineered by humanly-organized means.

I remember being in other meetings where there was a great attempt at the end to engineer "revival" through extended "altar calls." "Just one more song ...." "Come on, Christians, pray!" "Let's wait a little longer." "Okay, sing it once again." And on and on until it became painfully evident that nothing was truly happening but a lot of human striving to try to make something happen.

I don't for a minute doubt the sincerity of those involved in such meetings but we all need to learn more of God's ways — and HIS times. He is in charge. When HE moves it won't be because we strive and strive until we overcome His reluctance!

Other Signs

Other things that are often seen as signs of divine favor include: impressive buildings; big programs; large enthusiastic crowds; growth in organizations and movements; and the like. Do you really think Jesus is impressed with any of that? Much of the time all they are a "sign" of is human energy and ingenuity. And where the real engine is human energy and not Jesus building *his* church, demon energy and influence are not far behind.

Jesus wasn't the least impressed with the beautiful temple in Jerusalem. He pronounced judgment upon the religious establishment and prophesied the destruction of the temple of which they were so proud. In his ministry he never sought "quantity" but "quality." He sought only genuine believers, those to whom God had revealed who he was.

Do you think Jesus was distressed and upset when so many turned away in John 6? I don't. He understood what was happening. He knew that many of those who followed were simply sign or blessing seekers who had no real interest in truth. He never saw the crowds as evidence validating his ministry.

But many today do. They glory in the many outwardly-impressive aspects of their religious group believing them to be "signs" of God's favor. At the same time how many genuine followers of Jesus today gather at the risk of their lives in secret, meeting in caves, woods, and other remote places. What a contrast! There are going to be a lot of shocked people on judgment day.

Ministry Success

One area that merits particular comment concerns "success" in ministry and its evidence. Success in the minds of many is equated with "numbers," that is, a steady increase in the number of those professing faith in Christ. A church that is growing in membership is held up as an example of successful ministry, enjoying divine favor. It should be noted that by that measure Jesus was a great failure!

The pressure upon ministers for "results" begets much compromise and human effort. A wide range of means of attracting people is rationalized: "Let's get them in, then we'll get them saved." They are drawn in with entertainment, programs, groups catering to a wide range of interests, coffee bars, etc., etc.

Meanwhile the uncompromising message of the true gospel is "dumbed-down," soft-pedaled until all that is left is a God who wants to be your friend and help you fulfill your dreams. Just admit that you are a sinner and "accept" Jesus. Then check out our church programs and become active in whatever appeals to you.

What I have just described, sadly, does not overstate the situation in many places today. It no doubt *under*states it in many. But I fear that in many places the gospel, though it is not compromised to the degree some do, is nonetheless compromised through method and human effort and so produces a lot of false fruit.

Decisionism

Perhaps the prime example is what has been called "decisionism." Decisionism refers to the belief and practice of leading people through a simple "ABC" presentation of the gospel and then trying to get them to make a "decision" to "accept Jesus as their Savior." "Successful" ministers are those who become adept at preaching sermons and giving "altar calls" designed to lead people to "make decisions." Those who make such decisions are told that they are saved.

Does that mean that God has never saved people despite those methods? Of course not! But churches have been filled with lost church members by such methods despite appearances of success. One result is that many ministers today are far more "goat herders" than they are shepherds. Far too many of those that have been gathered are spiritual "goats." In order to maintain their "success," ministers feel great pressure to keep the goats from leaving and what few sheep there may be are starved in the process.

Where preachers employ such methods, and growth in membership and attendance results, that growth itself becomes a sign that confirms the methods used. Few there are who refuse to compromise, trusting God for genuine fruit in His time and way. Doing things God's way brings reproach in the eyes of men, but reward in heaven.

Manufacturing Christians

It ought to be clear from the scriptures that salvation is God's business and not something we can control. Many modern churches are essentially in the business of "manufacturing Christians"! It can't be done. The Bible is not a book of magic spells by which we can do the work of God! The so-called "sinner's prayer" is not a magic incantation that compels God to save anyone who says it.

I want to be very careful not to demean in any way those who may have been used of God to share the gospel in a way that has brought people to the feet of Jesus. But it is one thing for God to have prepared a heart, for Him to bring genuine conviction of sin and need, and for divinely-imparted faith to be exercised by a sinner in calling upon the name of Jesus for salvation. It is another for a person to be led by human effort to make a "decision." The key, obviously, is simple: is God truly at work or is the effort purely human?

My wife reminded me of something she experienced during our college days. She, together with a group of young people, had been trained to use what amounted to a gospel "script" designed to lead people to make "decisions." They went out one day on a beach to witness using that method. At the set time they all returned to count all the "decisions" they had obtained that day! I surely hope that in spite of it all, maybe God actually saved someone.

But the experience was an eye-opener for my wife. Something didn't feel right at all. I'm sure there was a measure of sincerity in the effort but no matter how sincere it may have been, no formula we can administer will produce children of God. And counting converts or "decisions" is surely a mark of something being wrong. It encourages further human effort as well as pride. And it becomes a "sign" that seemingly confirms that effort.

I remember something else that I encountered very early in pastoral ministry. I came into possession of a soul-winning, church-building program written by a "successful" minister somewhere. For a time I flirted with it until something didn't seem right. Church members were to be trained to go door-to-door to witness and invite people to church. Nothing wrong with that if God is in it.

But the program was constructed very much along the lines of a sales program, right down to a "gospel presentation" that was essentially a sales script designed to lead to a "sale." It attempted to bring the essential truths of the gospel down to something just about anybody could supposedly use to produce Christians. The part that stands out in my memory was the statement in the program to the effect that when the script was sincerely presented, the work of the Holy Spirit was *automatic*!

Seriously?! Who is in charge? It is one thing to be a yielded vessel, an instrument for God's purpose, trusting Him for genuine fruit. It is another to suppose that God has ceded control to us to push the right spiritual buttons and thereby invoke his automatic power. Does not the latter strongly resemble witchcraft?

Numbers?

What about numbers being a sign of spiritual success and blessing? I can't help but recall having heard many accounts from various mission fields that go something like this: a pioneer missionary would go with great sacrifice to some new field of ministry; he would faithfully pray and minister for decades and finally pass off the scene with little outward results to show for all his sacrifice; then, sometimes decades later, there would be a great ingathering by younger missionaries.

What happened? Was there something wrong with the earlier missionary? Was the harvest reaped by the later missionaries a sign of greater divine favor? Surely you know that the answer is no. The very nature of God's kingdom and man's way of doing things and evaluating his efforts are very different. Judgment day will make that apparent.

In John 4 we see the encounter between Jesus and the Samaritan "woman at the well." When the disciples return from buying food they are surprised that he is talking with her. He tells them that his food is to do the Father's will and that the "fields" are ready for harvest. Of course he was referring to a spiritual harvest.

In John 4:36-38 Jesus continued, "Even now the reaper draws his wages, even now he harvests the crop for eternal life, so that the sower and the reaper may be glad together. Thus the saying 'One sows and another reaps' is true. I sent you to reap what you have not worked for. Others have done the hard work, and you have reaped the benefits of their labor."

Do you get the picture? The kingdom of God is not about "results" as we tend to measure them. It is about doing the Father's will. There are seasons of planting and seasons of reaping. That is His business. Ours is just seeking and serving Him, not seeking "signs" or "results" that will impress others. I don't want to be among the many who will be shocked and dismayed on judgment day. Do you?

The question at hand concerns the active presence of Christ in his church. How do we know? Many equate his presence with a variety of "signs" as we have noted. True believers have a growing and very personal relationship with Christ that enables them increasingly to discern the difference between Christ and religion. True faith does not seek, nor does it depend upon signs that register in the sense realm. It rests upon something much deeper, much stronger, a hope that serves as an anchor for the soul. Hebrews 6:19.

In John 6 the crowds abandoned Jesus — but a small group including the twelve disciples stayed. Why? What did they have to hold them? Signs? Feelings? A popular leader? Did they understand Jesus' perplexing words? What then?

We find the answer in verse 65 where Jesus said, "No one can come to me unless the Father has enabled him." That is what enabled Peter to say, "Lord, to whom shall we go? You have the words of eternal life. We believe and know that you are the Holy One of God." Jesus had asked the disciples if they were going to leave too. Stripped of every natural thing that might have held them, he and the others were left with a simple, heaven-sent heart conviction of who Jesus was — and that was more than enough.

In John 10:14 Jesus said, "I am the good shepherd; I know my sheep and my sheep know me ...." In verse 27 he continued, "My sheep listen to my voice; I know them, and they follow me." He can make himself known to those who genuinely desire *him*. They know who he is!

Himself

I once remember hearing a minister — he happened to be of the Pentecostal variety — say, "You've got the doctrine; I've got the experience!" Of course there is *some* truth in that. Dead doctrine is no good. But there is something much better than "experience." I am from time to time reminded of the great hymn by A.B. Simpson entitled, "Himself." We may have, or think we have, many things, but when we truly have HIM, we have everything!

"Once it was the blessing, Now it is the Lord;

Once it was the feeling, Now it is His Word.

Once His gifts I wanted, Now the Giver own;

Once I sought for healing, Now Himself alone.

"Once 'twas painful trying, Now 'tis perfect trust;

Once a half salvation, Now the uttermost.

Once 'twas ceaseless holding, Now He holds me fast;

Once 'twas constant drifting, Now my anchor's cast.

"Once 'twas busy planning, Now 'tis trustful prayer;

Once 'twas anxious caring, Now He has the care.

Once 'twas what I wanted, Now what Jesus says;

Once 'twas constant asking, Now 'tis ceaseless praise.

"Once it was my working, His it hence shall be;
Once I tried to use Him, Now He uses me.
Once the power I wanted, Now the Mighty One;
Once for self I labored, Now for Him alone.

"Once I hoped in Jesus, Now I know He's mine;
Once my lamps were dying, Now they brightly shine.
Once for death I waited, Now His coming hail;
And my hopes are anchored, Safe within the vail."

And the chorus:
"All in all forever,
Jesus will I sing;
Everything in Jesus,
And Jesus everything."

Dr. Simpson has been gone from this earthly scene for nearly 100 years as I write this but never has this simple message been more needed by God's people as it is today.

As we continue we hope to further explore the true nature of the church, not just in theory, but as Paul sought to help real churches to recognize and confront Satan's attempts to invade and corrupt. I'm glad that the "bottom line" remains the promise of our Lord, "I will build my church, and the gates of Hades will not overcome it." Matt. 16:18. Hallelujah!

Chapter 9

Restaurant Religion

One of the greatest challenges throughout the Church's history has been avoiding assimilation by the world. Spiritually, our world is rightly labeled "Babylon," a system ruled over by Lucifer that stands in fierce opposition to the kingdom of God and of His Son, Jesus Christ. Babylon comes in many "flavors" but all express Lucifer's rebellion against God in one form or another.

In Col. 2:8 Paul wrote, "See to it that no one takes you captive through hollow and deceptive philosophy, which depends on human tradition and the basic principles of this world rather than on Christ." In the context he was concerned about religious teaching that turned people away from the full and complete salvation provided in Christ. Yet his warning applies equally well to any aspect of the world's wisdom with its ways of thinking and doing.

In spite of Paul's warning in Rom 12:2 not to "conform any longer to the pattern of this world" the church in America has in general been so compromised and absorbed into contemporary culture as to be almost indistinguishable from it. Many so-called "churches" are nothing more than organizations with a religious theme run by men. Christ's name is used but He has little or no influence over what goes on. The salt is no longer salty. Matt. 5:13.

Individualism

In reality every characteristic of deception we have noted thus far has its roots in the world and its god. There is one in particular that bears special mention at this point because it strikes at the very heart of what God intended for His Church. That characteristic is *individualism*.

Here are some dictionary definitions of individualism: "a social theory advocating the liberty, rights, or independent action of the individual"; "the principle or habit of or belief in independent thought or action"; "the pursuit of individual rather than common or collective interests; egoism."

Individualism is a very important part of American culture. This nation was born in part because of people seeking religious freedom from government tyranny. They fled to the new world to escape persecution from those who refused to allow them to worship God according to the dictates of their own consciences. The principles of freedom and individual rights were carefully enshrined in our constitution by our founding fathers.

Surely, most men would readily agree that in the realm of human affairs freedom is better than tyranny. I'm certainly thankful for the degree of freedom we still enjoy. Of course the rights of individuals must always be carefully balanced with the rights of society in general. We cannot allow murderers to run around murdering people in the name of individual liberty!

Who is in Control?

It is really about control. Am I in control of my life, free to do as I please, or do I live subject to the will of a king, a dictator, or some other form of governmental control? In human society those are basically the options and everywhere in the world we see the tension between those who want to impose their will on others and the desire of individuals to live in freedom.

Remember what we said earlier about the principle of "control" or "dominion." It flows from the rebellion of Lucifer against God. When he deceived our first parents in the garden that principle became a fundamental part of human nature. The temptation involved calling into question God's motives and therefore His trustworthiness and then promoting the idea that *they* should be as gods, that is, in control of their own lives and destinies.

One word describes all this: it is simply "rebellion." While this spirit of rebellion in man is what brings him into conflict with others it is really a rebellion against **God**. God's will is not paramount; **mine** is. **I** decide. **I** make the rules. **I** do as **I** please. And regardless of whether a particular society is a democracy, a dictatorship, a monarchy, or anything else, this spirit of rebellion is the driving force. It promotes self-will and seeks the interests of self above all else. It drives some to seek to control others and it drives others to live in a spirit of rebellious independence.

Is not this precisely what Jesus came to save us from? Isn't this what salvation is all about? And yet we see everywhere the ways of lost men carried over into religion. In some cases we see a spirit of control that subjugates people and in others we see self-willed individuals running around doing as they please, subject to no one's judgment but their own, and yet claiming to serve "Jesus." If they don't like it "here" they feel free to leave and run "there." They see this as their "right."

It would probably come as a shock to most Americans to hear that the Church of Jesus Christ is NOT a democracy! Of course it is not some form of human tyranny either. It doesn't matter where you are on the scale between democracy and tyranny: the real authority is human. *Men* are in charge. *Men* make the rules. *Men* decide. That may be how it is in the world but it is NOT how God's kingdom works. His purposes cannot be fulfilled by the ways of man.

Once God enters the picture there is another alternative to both the individualism and the tyranny that we see so much of, not only in society, but also in religion. That alternative goes right back to what Adam and Eve rebelled against in the beginning: **divine authority**. **God** is the creator. **He** makes the rules. It is **His** will and purpose that will prevail. Adam and Eve lost confidence in God's loving rule and we see the results of their rebellion everywhere in our world. It is only in heart surrender to divine authority that we return to a proper relationship with our Creator.

Personal and Private

Yet it is right here that Satan deceives. He promotes the idea that serving God and walking with Jesus is such a personal and private thing that the rebellion of individualism is untouched. Self reigns. It may be religious yet the real authority is "self." It is religion according to *me,* according to *my* understanding and convictions. No one has the right to tell me what to do — or even to suggest that I am wrong. *Jesus is leading me!* Is He?

How well this fits in with relativism of modern thought where there is no such thing as objective truth. Each one is entitled to his own "truth." And woe to anyone who dares to claim that they have THE truth in any area of life. "How dare you claim that you are right and that I am wrong. You are intolerant and I am offended!" What in the world would they do with Jesus!?

Religious Individualism

We see an example of religious individualism in Deuteronomy 12. Moses was instructing the generation of Israelites who would ultimately conquer and settle Canaan. He refers to the religious practices of the heathen with their many gods and many places of worship. In verses 4-5 he says, "You must not worship the Lord your God in their way. But you are to seek the place the Lord your God will choose from among all your tribes to put his Name there for his dwelling." Remember that last part about God establishing a "dwelling."

In verses 8-9 Moses says something rather telling: "You are not to do as we do here today, everyone as he sees fit, since you have not yet reached the resting place and the inheritance the Lord your God is giving you." It wasn't just that the heathen did as they pleased when it came to religion; the Israelites did as well! Yet aren't Moses' words a pretty good description of how the modern church world does — *"everyone as he sees fit"*? And yet the Lord was telling the Israelites that it *wasn't* to be that way. **He** would establish a place where they were to come and worship the way **He** prescribed.

It is a common saying in the church world: "Attend the church of your choice." That sounds good — and it fits in well with our American idea of individual rights and liberties. It is based on the idea that there are good churches everywhere and each one of us should simply choose the one we prefer. Never mind the fact that they differ dramatically from one another. Just try them out and find one you like. You choose one you prefer; I'll do the same; and it'll be just fine. God's cool with that. We're all serving the same Jesus, heading the same direction. Are we?

I'm so glad that the Lord is merciful in the midst of the division and confusion of the religious world. He won't lose even one of His own but to suppose that *this order of things* is somehow OK with Him is simply not so. In the scenario above, *who is doing the choosing?* Are not individuals choosing based on **their** personal ideas and preferences? Where do those preferences come from? What happened to the Lordship of Christ? Is He not in charge? Is it Christ that has established all this division and confusion — or does God perhaps have a different vision? Should we not seek Him for that? Will Christ return for a carnal divided church? Is that His plan?

The Restaurant Principle

Recently I was meditating on this and the Lord quickened a simple picture of what most religion is like in His eyes. Think of the restaurant business. In a restaurant, people — customers — pay money for ready-to-eat food. That food may be anything from a simple snack like ice cream to a full meal. It might be eaten in the restaurant or it might perhaps be carried out to be eaten somewhere else. A restaurant is different from a grocery store or a market where people buy food to prepare at home. A restaurant is designed for people who simply want the convenience of exchanging money for food that someone else has prepared.

Since people have a wide variety of personal tastes in food there is naturally a similar variety of restaurants who cater to those tastes. Some people are happy with so-called "fast food." They lead busy lives and are glad for prepared food that tastes reasonably good, is cheap, and doesn't take up a lot of time from their busy schedules.

Other people are looking for more out of their dining experience. One important part of that is the menu. What *kind* of food is served. Of course the human family has developed a great variety of tasty styles of food and that is reflected in restaurants. Some people like Italian food, others Chinese, others Indian, others French, and so on. Some are vegetarians while others can't live without their steak and potatoes. We could easily spend a lot of time listing just some of the kinds of food people go to restaurants to eat. But you get the point.

Some restaurant-goers want the same thing all the time and others like the variety they can get by visiting different places. Cafeteria type restaurants are popular because you can just go to the food bar and pick what you happen to want that day.

Of course the menu is not all that is important. While it is true that some people just want to grab some food to eat on the run others are looking for a total dining "experience." Not only do they want just the right food; they also demand a certain kind of atmosphere in which to enjoy it. It certainly wouldn't be appropriate to serve a fancy steak dinner next to a garbage can in the alley! Atmosphere matters.

Some want a quiet place where they can eat in peace. Others like to be in a noisy crowd. The kind of music plays an important part. It might be classical music or it might be loud rock music or country music.

One popular restaurant type in the United States is the "diner" where customers either sit in a booth or on a stool at a counter. They are modeled after the old dining cars found on trains. Diner type restaurants typically cater to working class people who dress casually. They often have brassy friendly waitresses who call their customers "darling" and who yell out orders to the kitchen.

Other dining customers would turn up their noses at such a low-class place. They want something fancy, sophisticated, and of course, expensive. Diners are expected to dress up and make reservations. Often part of what draws the customers is a famous and talented chef who knows how to prepare real gourmet fare.

In short, restaurants are as varied as the customers they hope to attract. And in our increasingly connected world you can find an amazing variety most anywhere. I've had the privilege of traveling to the Philippines on several occasions and can recall eating in an Italian restaurant, a German restaurant, and a Chinese restaurant, as well as enjoying foods from many parts of the world in hotel cafeteria type restaurants. I also recall eating there at McDonald's, Kentucky Fried Chicken, and no doubt others that don't come to mind. I even had a "Cajun" dish at one restaurant (at least that's what they said it was!).

The Customer is King

Now think with me for a moment: in the restaurant business, who is in charge? Is it not the customer? You may have heard the expression, "The customer is king," and that is certainly true. A restaurant owner stays in business and prospers because he provides customers with what they want. Suppose a businessman said, "I'm not going to do that anymore; I'm going to give my customers what they *need*, not what they want." How long would he stay in business? Not long! His customers would simply stop coming and go somewhere else.

But is not religion like that? Is it not "customer-driven"? Are not even some good men held hostage by the religious tastes of their "customers"?

Think of Paul's warning to Timothy in 2 Tim. 4:1-4 — "In the presence of God and of Christ Jesus, who will judge the living and the dead, and in view of his appearing and his kingdom, I give you this charge: Preach the Word; be prepared in season and out of season; correct, rebuke and encourage — with great patience and careful instruction. For the time will come when men will not put up with sound doctrine. Instead, to suit their own desires, they will gather around them a great number of teachers to say what their itching ears want to hear. They will turn their ears away from the truth and turn aside to myths."

What would happen if real men of God suddenly stepped into every pulpit in America and did what Paul said? Do you think the result would be any different than what happened when Stephen told the truth to the Jewish Sanhedrin in Acts 7? They might not be literally stoned but the spirit behind the reaction would be exactly the same. Don't you dare say anything about my religion!

Satan has largely corrupted the American church by turning it into a customer-driven enterprise. The customer is king. Pastors are hired and fired based on their ability to attract and satisfy the "customers." Preaching style and ability, worship style, meeting style, programs and activities, personalities all play their part in providing the total religious experience. People want to leave with a good feeling about themselves, that everything is OK with them and God. If they don't get what they want in one place they will run to another.

Self Reigns

Is this not individualism in action? The rebellion of self-will has been clothed with religion and passed off as real Christianity. Multitudes call Jesus "Lord" but they live and act in rebellion. Isn't this exactly what Jesus spoke of in Matt. 7:21-23? He said, "Not everyone who says to me, 'Lord, Lord,' will enter the kingdom of heaven, but only he who does the will of my Father who is in heaven. Many will say to me on that day, 'Lord, Lord, did we not prophesy in your name, and in your name drive out demons and perform many miracles?' Then I will tell them plainly, 'I never knew you. Away from me, you evildoers!'"

The spirit of Babylon is designed by Satan to protect and even to promote "self." The Spirit of God through the true gospel of Jesus Christ *confronts* self and brings about godly sorrow and genuine repentance. In salvation "self" dies and Christ lives in its place. The preaching of the cross never compromises with self. It never seeks to please men but only God. The stakes are too high. Men's souls hang in the balance.

In religion "self" reigns. Preachers cannot afford to offend the "customers." They might leave — and take their contributions with them. How would the mortgage payments on the big new church building be met? The ways of religion have a million insidious ways of standing squarely in the way of a true work of God.

Rock Stars

One interesting characteristic of modern religion needs to be particularly pointed out. Often we see gifted preachers, teachers, or singers become celebrities, sometimes almost "rock stars." Some of these have a measure of genuine ministry. What is that about? I'm glad for anyone that the Lord in mercy reaches for himself but this celebrity culture is often of a different sort. Just as those Jesus described as *calling* him Lord were not in fact true followers so it is with many people today. People are able to "celebrate" truth and enjoy emotional religious experiences yet never truly bow to Him who is **the truth**. *Self is never conquered.*

Consider this biblical example. Surely everyone would agree that Ezekiel was a man of God, a prophet chosen of God to preach hard truth in a challenging time. Yet God spoke to Ezekiel on one occasion to explain what the real deal was with some of his listeners. It surely would have been natural for Ezekiel to suppose that people coming to hear him were genuine seekers of truth but that wasn't the case. Consider what the Lord told him.

Ezek. 33:30-32 — "As for you, son of man, your countrymen are talking together about you by the walls and at the doors of the houses, saying to each other, 'Come and hear the message that has come from the Lord.' My people come to you, as they usually do, and sit before you to listen to your words, but they do not put them into practice. With their mouths they express devotion, but their hearts are greedy for unjust gain. Indeed, to them you are nothing more than one who sings love songs with a beautiful voice and plays an instrument well, for they hear your words but do not put them into practice."

Think about what the Lord was saying! These people were in such a hardened spiritual condition that they could sit before a true prophet of God and basically treat what he said as entertainment, as a performance. Is it really that different in our day? And how much of purported ministry in our day really is a ministry of the Spirit and how much is just a subtle form of religious entertainment? and "customer-driven" at that? God help us!

When Persecution Comes

When persecution comes — and it will — just how much of the American religious scene will simply evaporate? It isn't real. Millions of people have been begotten in a system that protects self-will at all costs. They are lost and don't know it. What God intended when Christ began to build his church and what American religion has largely become are two very different things. Many cry out for revival and revival is a wonderful thing but God's heart cries out for something much deeper than revival. What He longs for cannot be fulfilled in "the system." It can only happen "outside the camp." It can only be engineered by Christ himself. It can never happen while individualism reigns. Christ is Lord and self must give way to his Lordship.

In Chapter 6 we began to speak of the nature of the church as God sees it. It consists of the company of the redeemed who literally share the life of God, with each other, and with the Father and His Son. It is not an organization but a living organism. Its members have given up their lives to possess God's life. They have bowed to Christ as Lord. Yet it is not just about their relationship with God but also with *each other*. God has a vision laid out in His Word for the church, not just in eternity, but **here in this world**. To the extent that we have declared that to be impossible and have just accepted the current state of things as OK we have embraced deception. Satan is lying to us.

Chapter 10

God's Plan for the Church

Paul's understanding of God's vision and plan for the church is not something he learned in school, nor was it the product of his own diligent study. He did not even learn it at the feet of those who were apostles before him. It was very simply something God supernaturally revealed to him. God singled out Paul to communicate His heart and thus it is no accident that Paul was the human author of so much of the New Testament.

It is easy in his writings to sense not only *his* passion on the subject but *God's* as well. There is everywhere expressed a burning desire that his readers "get it," that they understand and experience the greatness of God's purpose.

The Mystery of Christ

In Ephesians 3 Paul uses an interesting expression: "the mystery of Christ." In verse 3 he notes the fact that this mystery was "made known to me by revelation." It should be obvious from his words that what Paul knew could **only** be known by divine revelation. It has nothing whatever to do with how smart we are, how sincere, or how hard we study. When it comes to divine mysteries we are completely at the mercy of God. Unless He chooses to reveal something to us we remain in ignorance. Would that we were always honest about what we don't know!

Paul summarizes this divine mystery in verse 6: "This mystery is that through the gospel the Gentiles are heirs together with Israel, members together of one body, and sharers together in the promise in Christ Jesus."

In part this mystery addressed a very important first century issue, that of the place of Jew and Gentile in the plan of God. In Christ this distinction has been forever destroyed as Paul so clearly expresses in Eph. 2:11-22. The "barrier," the "dividing wall of hostility," was "destroyed" (verse 14). Access to God and citizenship in His kingdom is now equally available to all through Christ and his death on the cross. It has nothing to do with national or ethnic background.

One New Man

In Eph. 2:15-16 Paul writes, "His purpose was to create in himself one new man out of the two, thus making peace, and in this one body to reconcile both of them to God through the cross, by which he put to death their hostility." Note the interesting expressions of oneness and wholeness he uses: "one new man" and "one body." It is not simply that God sought many new men but **one new man**. He sees things differently than we do.

Notice also that this one new man was *created* and that this creation took place *in Christ Jesus*. Such language highlights the fact that this is entirely a supernatural work of God, just as much as the original creation was when God spoke the universe into existence.

A lot more happened when Jesus was raised from the dead than simply the resurrection of one person from physical death. It is not just Jesus Christ the individual that had Paul excited. It is what was **in him**. In him a new creation was born. We were there! All that we will ever be was there in him just awaiting the day when we would by God's grace be brought to the hope of the gospel and become partakers of the life that was in him.

Remember John 12:23-24 where Jesus said, "The hour has come for the Son of Man to be glorified. I tell you the truth, unless a kernel of wheat falls to the ground and dies, it remains only a single seed. But if it dies, it produces many seeds." A seed contains all of the future generations that will result from the life that is in it. In particular the life that was in Jesus contained the Church he died to redeem, right down to the very last member. If you are His then **you** were there.

Alive With Christ

In Eph. 2:4-7 Paul writes, "But because of his great love for us, God, who is rich in mercy, made us alive with Christ even when we were dead in transgressions — it is by grace you have been saved. And God raised us up with Christ and seated us with him in the heavenly realms in Christ Jesus, in order that in the coming ages he might show the incomparable riches of his grace, expressed in his kindness to us in Christ Jesus."

Notice the way he puts it. God "made us alive **with Christ**." "God raised us up **with Christ**." He also "seated us **with him** in the heavenly realms **in Christ**." All of this extends into the eternal future when He shows us "the incomparable riches of his grace, expressed in his kindness to us **in Christ Jesus**."

When were we made alive? When Christ was. When were we raised up? When he was. Where are we as a result? In the heavenly realms. How? In Christ. If you hand someone a box you hand them not only the box but whatever is *in* that box. Everything that happened to Jesus Christ happened to all of God's people because they were "in him."

If you go to a tree nursery and buy a young fruit tree to plant in your yard you buy not only the young tree as it is but also every leaf and every branch it will ever produce. They are already there — in the tree. Leaves and branches are not special options bought separately from the tree! And every part of that developing tree plays a part both in its growth and in the fruit that is produced.

For Us Who Believe

That is why Paul wanted his readers to understand the greatness of what God did in Christ — because we were there. In Eph. 1:18-21 he writes, "I pray also that the eyes of your heart may be enlightened in order that you may know the hope to which he has called you, the riches of his glorious inheritance in the saints, and his incomparably great power for us who believe. That power is like the working of his mighty strength, which he exerted in Christ when he raised him from the dead and seated him at his right hand in the heavenly realms, far above all rule and authority, power and dominion, and every title that can be given, not only in the present age but also in the one to come."

This is not mere abstract theology, interesting to think about but not really connected with everyday life. If we would see things as God sees them we would see that the awesome things He did in His Son were done "**for us who believe**" and were meant to give us a solid foundation of hope not only for the eternal future but here in this world as well. No devil in hell can withstand or undo what God has given us in His Son!

Christ?

What do you think of when you hear the word "Christ"? I daresay that most would think of *Jesus* Christ, the individual, the Son of God who once walked the shores of Galilee and who now reigns on high. That is true enough but God's vision is larger. In Eph. 1:22-23 we read, "And God placed all things under his feet and appointed him to be head over everything for the church, which is his body, the fullness of him who fills everything in every way."

Christ's power and exaltation is not just for his own benefit; it is "**for the church.**" More than that it is "for the church, **which is his body.**" But even that doesn't quite paint the picture. This body is "**the fullness of him....**" What does that mean? Put crudely it simply means that the church is the

rest of him. He is not complete without the Church any more than your head is complete without your body.

If I were to meet you and all I saw was your head I might well ask, "Where is the rest of you?" I am sure that the Father welcomed His Son back to glory with great joy and yet His great heart longed for the day when the "rest of him" would likewise be glorified. We tend to see Christ and the church as separate things but God doesn't see them that way.

Paul didn't either. We can see the roots of Paul's understanding in the very moment he met Christ on the Damascus road experience. Knocked from his horse by a blinding light he heard a voice say, "Saul, Saul, why do you persecute me?" His response was to ask, "Who are you, Lord?" The answer came, "I am Jesus whom you are persecuting?"

Of course in his mind it was the *followers* of Jesus who were being persecuted but in the mind of Jesus his union with those followers was so complete that the persecution was actually against *him personally*. Thus was Saul, later known as Paul, introduced very early to the reality of Christ's living union with his Church.

The Oneness of Christ's Body

In 1 Cor. 12:12-13 Paul writes, "The body is a unit, though it is made up of many parts; and though all its parts are many, they form one body. So it is with Christ. For we were all baptized by one Spirit into one body — whether Jews or Greeks, slave or free — and we were all given the one Spirit to drink." So *what* is with Christ? **"Christ" is a many-membered body.** *Jesus* Christ is the Head — but the church is the body. It is only *together* that we have the entire Christ as God sees things. Of course the church is nothing in itself and has nothing to boast of except its glorious Head.

Notice that word "unit." Paul is not writing to emphasize the "many parts" but rather the "unit," the simple fact that those parts make up "one body." In the minds of so many the "body of Christ" is a somewhat vague mystical thing perhaps illustrating the variety of gifts and abilities in individual believers but little else. While it is true that every true born-again believer is a member of the body of Christ it is also true that in Paul's teaching the body of Christ was meant to be a practical and local reality.

People weren't baptized into a mystical body and left to do as they pleased. He said to the Corinthian believers, "Now you are the body of Christ, and each one of you is a part of it." 1 Cor. 12:27-28. He didn't say, "You are *part of* the body"; he said, "You are *the* body of Christ." They were the living, breathing, body of Christ in that location, members one of another, every part vital.

Every part of your body, including your head, is vitally connected to every other part. All of the parts share the very same life. There is a total interdependence in the relationship of those parts to each other. Every part contributes something to the whole according to its designed function and every part receives what it needs as all the other parts do the same. Every part takes its direction from the head.

How well would your body function if all its parts declared their rights to independence?!

And it wasn't just the *spirits* of believers that were somehow mystically joined to other believers. The union also involved their *bodies*. In 1 Cor. 6 Paul warns the believers against sexual immorality. He tells them why in verse 15 — "Do you not know that your bodies are members of Christ himself?" Think about what he is saying there. Your bodies are actually part of Christ! They are meant to express his life even as Jesus expressed the life of his Father through his body.

What Satan Fears

But Jesus was a complete expression of the Father. Individually we are *not* complete expressions of Christ. It is only in a living practical union that the world can see him come in the flesh as God intended. It is this corporate expression that Satan fears. He *loves* the "mystical" universal body since it is little more than an idea and no real threat to his kingdom.

Being joined to the mystical body is sort of like a man being married to a mystical wife! No matter what her imagined virtues may be she will never cook his breakfast nor bear his children!

In the body of Christ "separateness" — which is really rebellious independence — gives way to the oneness of being part of Christ. The smallness of self dies that the greatness of Christ may live and find expression in the earth.

God's Temple

In Eph. 2:19-22 Paul gives us a different picture of the church as God sees it, but one that conveys the same essential message. "Consequently, you are no longer foreigners and aliens, but fellow citizens with God's people and members of God's household, built on the foundation of the apostles and prophets, with Christ Jesus himself as the chief cornerstone. In him the whole building is joined together and rises to become a holy temple in the Lord. And in him you too are being built together to become a dwelling in which God lives by his Spirit."

And so Paul moves from "one new man" and "one body" to a "whole building" that is "joined together" and is being "built together." The common theme is clear: there is a very real and practical "togetherness" that God seeks. He is building a home for Himself.

Paul's thought here is not something separate from the verses that precede it. It is connected by the word "*consequently.*" God's purpose to construct a house for Himself is a direct consequence of the reconciliation of one body to God through the cross.

Not Just in Heaven

Reconciliation with a holy God is a wonderful thing but it is not an end in itself. God has something particular in mind. That something has practical implications. It implies some very important things about the life of God's people *now* — here on earth — and not just in heaven someday. The church does not suddenly leap from individualism to "templehood" merely by being transported to heaven. Rather it is "joined together" *here* and *"rises to become* a holy temple." What **will be** is our destiny. But there is a God-ordained process that leads to that destiny.

Suppose you decide to build a house and at great cost you purchase the finest building materials money can buy. But suppose those fine building materials are never cut, fitted, and fastened together by a skilled builder according to a good master plan. Where would you live? If someone were to ask you where you lived would you point to the scattered materials and say, "There ... and there ... and, well, everywhere!"? What good would that be?

In the same way materials that are separate and scattered do not a temple make. They must surrender their separateness to the Master Builder and be shaped and fitted together according to God's design.

Who is this Master Builder? Did not Jesus say, "I will build my church"? Matt. 16:18. The problem is that many zealous religious people have tried to build Jesus a church — according to *their* design. God's plan by contrast is for Jesus to call a people to the kingdom through the gospel, build them together as a body, practically, locally, as a place where he can dwell and express himself in the earth.

No man can engineer such a thing. We can only repent and cry out to God to bring it about and to reveal our place in the body. There we look to Christ as Head and submit ourselves one to another, ministering one to another according to the gifts and abilities Christ the Head gives.

Christ in heaven is wonderful; but it is Christ in his body that God seeks. The vision of God's heart has been subverted by religious tradition and the zealous efforts of men. The rebellion of individualism has been justified by an appeal to the concept of the "mystical" body of Christ. While God's vision is explained away as impractical and unrealistic the religious machinery grinds on. Has not the deceiver been at work?

Chapter 11

The Principle of Promise

In the book of Romans Paul sets forth the wonders of the gospel which he calls "the power of God for the salvation of everyone who believes: first for the Jew, then for the Gentile." Rom. 1:16. Paul's own religious background had led him to believe that God had given the law of Moses so that Jews could earn their own salvation through obedience to it, that is, through works. When the revelation of Jesus Christ came it turned his world — and his understanding — upside down. Not only was salvation NOT earned by one's works; it was for EVERYONE, not just Jews!

In Chapter 4 Paul uses Abraham as an example of salvation by faith rather than works and in the process paints a picture of how God deals with man down through the ages — including us. There is a word used several times in this chapter that has often come to my mind of late. I believe it is a real key. That word is "promise."

Because of sin the world was under the power of darkness. It was into that darkness that the God of all grace came. He spoke to a man named Abram who lived among a family of idol worshippers. But God's words to him were not a demand that Abram live up to a moral standard and thereby qualify himself for a divine blessing. Rather, the heart of God's words to him was a **promise**.

God's Promise

In Gen. 12:2-3 we read that promise: "I will make you into a great nation and I will bless you; I will make your name great, and you will be a blessing. I will bless those who bless you, and whoever curses you I will curse; and all peoples on earth will be blessed through you." What God commanded him to do is recorded in verse 1: "Leave your country, your people and your father's household and go to the land I will show you."

Abram did not **earn** the blessing by obeying the Lord. Rather he demonstrated an obedience that was consistent with **believing the promise**. Thus he obtained the blessing not *by* works, nor by so-called faith *without* works (James 2:14-26) but by faith *that* works (Gal. 5:6). The real heart of the matter was his faith in God.

This is made very clear in Genesis 15. God's promise to Abram (later called Abraham) involved his becoming a great nation. This presented a very real practical problem! Abram was childless and getting old fast. Sarah could no longer bear children. How was such a thing to be?

According to the custom of the times a servant of his named Eliezer of Damascus stood to inherit his estate and that didn't fit God's promise so he asked the Lord about it. It was on this occasion that the Lord assured him that a son coming from his own body would be his heir. He then told Abram to count the stars and said that his offspring would be like them in number.

Abram Believed the Lord

Gen. 15:6 tells us simply, "Abram believed the Lord, and he credited it to him as righteousness." Long before the law of Moses this former idol worshipper was declared by a holy God to be righteous. On what ground? His works? No! His faith.

And I believe we can see in his life that his faith was deeper than simply believing a *promise*. Rather, he believed the *One that was making the promise*. He believed **the Lord**. In other words, his confidence in God was such that it didn't matter *what* He said, Abram believed it.

There is a simple word for that. It is the word "trust." Abram's trust in God was so pure that, for example, when God later told him to offer the son of promise as a sacrifice he didn't hesitate to obey. That is a picture of absolute trust. He may have had his ideas as to how God would work it out but the bottom line is that he simply obeyed. The Lord finally stepped in when it became obvious that he would not allow anything to stand in the way of obedience, not even sacrificing the promised heir.

Is that not what was lost in the beginning? Eve, and then Adam, were seduced into believing the lie that God could not be trusted, that He was holding them back, keeping them from their true destiny, no doubt for selfish reasons. Thus the very essence of a restored relationship between man and God is **trust**. From Abraham's day to this God has been at work calling a people back to a relationship of absolute trust, unfolding a purpose that reaches from eternity past into the eternal future.

Trust and Obey

How simple! A divine promise fulfilled through trust and obedience. "Trust and obey." It has a nice ring to it, don't you think! Say, that would make a great hymn!

It should be obvious that a divine promise is the only thing that will fulfill God's purpose. Sin has rendered man incapable of helping himself — even if he wanted to! Rom. 3:10-12.

Abraham's natural condition was just as hopeless. He couldn't even produce a son let alone nations. And he surely couldn't engineer a blessing for all nations. What God promised Abraham could ONLY be done by God. All Abraham could do was to believe and cooperate through obedience.

Even so, Abraham tried to help God out but the result was Ishmael who could never inherit the promise. I'm glad for every natural child of Ishmael who has entered into the promise through faith in Christ but the unfolding of God's plan came through Isaac. God had fixed it so that only a miracle would avail. Abraham was as helpless to fulfill God's purposes through his own efforts as we are today.

We find these wonderful words in Rom. 4:18-24 — "Against all hope, Abraham in hope believed and so became the father of many nations, just as it had been said to him, 'So shall your offspring be.' Without weakening in his faith, he faced the fact that his body was as good as dead — since he was about a hundred years old — and that Sarah's womb was also dead. Yet he did not waver through unbelief regarding the promise of God, but was strengthened in his faith and gave glory to God, being fully persuaded that God had power to do what he had promised. This is why 'it was credited to him as righteousness.' The words 'it was credited to him' were written not for him alone, but also for us, to whom God will credit righteousness — for us who believe in him who raised Jesus our Lord from the dead." (I wonder how many of us today have "faced the fact" that we cannot help God out!)

God's Heir

Thank God for righteousness but there is much more to it than that. In Rom. 4:13 Paul speaks of God's promise to Abraham "that he would be heir of the world." In other words, God has a great inheritance He longs to share with men. Out of all the people in the world in Abraham's day God chose Abraham to be His heir. Thus the promise reached far beyond this present evil world into the one to come.

Abraham's Children

But of course the inheritance was not just for one man but for all of Abraham's children. Who are they? In many places Paul makes it plain that the children God had in mind for this inheritance were children of Abraham's **faith** and not his body. They include a remnant of his natural descendants who believe but also Gentiles who come to faith in Christ. Rom. 4:16, 9:6-9, 22-27, Gal. 3:26-29, 4:28.

In the unfolding of God's promise He did indeed deal with the nation of Israel in spite of its general unbelief, but the fulfillment of that promise was yet to come in Christ. The law of Moses was a temporary covenant that was intended to lead them to the One to come. For the remnant it did just that and they entered in.

In Gal. 3:19 we read, "What, then, was the purpose of the law? It was added because of transgressions until the Seed to whom the promise referred had come." Paul continues in Gal. 3:21-22, "Is the law, therefore, opposed to the promises of God? Absolutely not! For if a law had been given that could impart life, then righteousness would certainly have come by the law. But the Scripture declares that the whole world is a prisoner of sin, so that what was promised, being given through faith in Jesus Christ, might be given to those who believe."

That brings every true follower of Jesus Christ directly into the stream of God's eternal purpose. What God began in Abraham continues in us today. The complete fulfillment of that promise lies ahead of us, as sure as the One Who promised. Heb. 6:13-20 reminds us that our trust is in One that cannot lie.

As we have said, Abraham's immediate concern was having a son, something humanly impossible, but no problem at all to God. But Hebrews indicates that in some sense the vision of Abraham, Isaac, and Jacob reached far beyond such immediate issues. Heb. 11:10 tells us that Abraham "was looking forward to the city with foundations, whose architect and builder is God."

Heb. 11:13-16 continues, "All these people were still living by faith when they died. They did not receive the things promised; they only saw them and welcomed them from a distance. And they admitted that they were aliens and strangers on earth. People who say such things show that they are looking for a country of their own. If they had been thinking of the country they had left, they would have had opportunity to return. Instead, they were longing for a better country — a heavenly one. Therefore God is not ashamed to be called their God, for he has prepared a city for them." And for us as well.

Impossibility

Every generation of believers from Abraham's day to this has faced its own particular impossibilities. Not only Abraham but also his son Isaac needed divine intervention just to produce one heir, let alone a nation! The Israelites were slaves in Egypt, the mightiest nation of its day. They faced walled cities and giants in their conquest of the promised land. The persistent wickedness of Israel and the resulting divine judgment down through the centuries seemed to the small believing remnant to be an insurmountable problem.

The Lord repeatedly sent prophets, not only to denounce the sins of the nation, but also to encourage the remnant concerning the redemption that was to come. Elijah, one of the mightiest prophets, was so discouraged on one occasion that he prayed to die since he believed himself to be the only one left who was serving the Lord. But the Lord told Elijah that

He had preserved 7000 men who had not bowed the knee to Baal.

God's purpose unfolded throughout centuries of darkness and seeming impossibility not because of human effort but through His own mighty hand. **God** preserved that remnant. No devil in hell could stand in His way. And then Christ came!

A Foundation for Righteousness

I pointed out earlier that Abram was declared righteous, not through some kind of self-righteous effort, but through faith alone. How could a holy God do that? He could do that because what no man could do for himself, God did through Christ. We were helpless prisoners of sin. So God acted to put away our sin by punishing His own Son on our behalf. Justice demanded the death of every sinner. That justice was satisfied through Christ's death in our place. God is free to justify anyone who responds to the gospel in repentance and faith. His justification of Abraham was based on Christ's sacrifice to come. That was the essence of the promise, the blessing that was for all nations. God can deal with our *need*. He seeks our *trust*.

On the day of Pentecost God poured out His Spirit as He had promised. Peter stood up with great power to explain to the crowds gathered for the Feast of Pentecost that what was happening was the fulfillment of God's promises to Israel through the prophets. He boldly proclaimed the resurrection of Christ not only as a fact to which they were witnesses but also as a promise proclaimed through David in Psalm 16. He brought his message into focus with these penetrating words in Acts 2:36 – "Therefore let all Israel be assured of this: God has made this Jesus, whom you crucified, both Lord and Christ."

The Spirit of God was present not only to anoint Peter but also to directly convict the hearers and they cried out wanting to know what to do. In verse 38 he replied, "Repent and be baptized, every one of you, in the name of Jesus Christ for the forgiveness of your sins. And you will receive the gift of the Holy Spirit."

A Promise For All

I find it very interesting and significant that in verse 39 Peter uses the word "promise." He says, "The promise is for you and your children and for all who are far off — for all whom the Lord our God will call." The blessing promised to Abraham had come. It was now time to proclaim the hope of the gospel — the good news — not only to Israel but to all the world.

At every stage of the unfolding of God's purpose to call out a people for Himself the principle of "promise" applies. What is needed to fulfill that purpose is **something only God can do**. The very best we can do is to cooperate with His purpose through trust and obedience; there is absolutely no human effort that will avail.

Many understand that to be true when it comes to the salvation of the individual but how much do we understand it to be true with respect to the building of Christ's church and its preparation for all that is to come? After all, Christ did not tell us to build him a church; he said he would do it.

And numerous scriptures promise us that what has been begun will be finished. See Phil. 1:6, Heb. 11:38-12:2, and Eph. 1:7-10, for example. Rom. 8:28-30 even uses the past tense concerning the ultimate climax of God's purpose when it says in verse 30, "those he justified he also glorified." In God's mind it has already been done! What a glorious hope it is to which we have been called!

Nearing the End

Increasingly, believers in our day have the sense that we are nearing that climax, the end of the age, and the coming again of our Lord Jesus Christ. What a day that will be! When God is through and His purpose fulfilled His people will be forever free from the power of sin and death (Rev. 21:4-7), radiant in glory (1 Peter 5:1, 10), shining like the sun (Matt. 13:43), with bodies like the one Jesus has (Phil. 3:20-21), living in a brand new world (2 Peter 3:13), full fellowship with God restored (Rev. 21:3).

In the Meantime

But what about until that day? What do we do in the meantime? What can we expect? What will the state of God's people be when Christ returns? How do we prepare? Do

God's promises have anything for us *now*? How can we be aligned with *God's* purpose?

As we survey the religious landscape of today it is evident that there are a great variety of answers to these questions. Satan ever works to obscure truth and misdirect God's people. His efforts to deceive have no doubt affected us all more than we might care to admit.

Many today loudly proclaim their expectation that Christ is coming "at any moment" to "rapture" the church. Well ... I hope he does! He won't get any argument from me. But that raises a lot of questions.

The church, particularly in America, is mostly asleep, carnal, immature, divided, almost indistinguishable from the world, and largely laughed at by Satan and much of society. Is *that* what Christ is coming for? The church began at Pentecost with a bang; will it end with a whimper? Really? Are we destined to go out like a dog with its tail between its legs, a far cry from the heavenly calling set forth in scripture? Will God's wonderful promises go unfulfilled? Will Christ pull his people out in defeat?

Something in me cries out, "No!" I am very aware that simply looking at the situation can easily provoke a sense of futility. "Nothing can be done. That's just the way it is. The best we can hope for is that there will be pockets of revival here and there from time to time and that Jesus will come to rescue us and straighten out the mess." But then I look into scripture and get a very different sense.

I read the words of Paul, for example, in Eph. 3:10-11, where he speaks of God in these words: "His intent was that now, through the church, the manifold wisdom of God should be made known to the rulers and authorities in the heavenly realms, according to his eternal purpose which he accomplished in Christ Jesus our Lord." God's demonstration to those rulers and authorities was pretty impressive in the beginning but what about now? Was that it? Paul wrote those words long after Pentecost.

He prayed in verse 19, "that you may be filled to the measure of all the fullness of God." That's a pretty difficult thing for you and me to imagine, isn't it! But Paul didn't stop there. Eph, 3:20-21 says, "Now to him who is able to do immeasurably more than all we ask or imagine, according to his power that is at work within us, to him be glory in the church and in Christ Jesus throughout all generations, for ever and ever! Amen."

The obvious reason as to why such things are hard to imagine is that what we see appears to present insurmountable obstacles. But let's not forget how God's purpose unfolds. It begins with a promise. The promise concerns things that are totally impossible to us but as certain as the One making the promise. The appropriate human response is to believe. That belief is expressed as total trust on the one hand and obedience on the other. In other words, we simply do our part and God takes care of what is impossible.

Everything in God's Time

The details of how and when He acts are up to Him. Abraham waited 25 years for the promised son. He came when it was God's time. In God's time Israel was delivered from slavery in Egypt. Not one second before! Gal. 4:4 tells us that "when the time had fully come, God sent his Son...." The climax of the ages will likewise be "put into effect when the times will have reached their fulfillment." Eph. 1:10.

God has His own schedule. Lazarus had been dead and buried four days and Jesus seemed to be "late" but in the purpose of God he was exactly on time! Raising a man from the dead after four days was a much greater miracle than simply preventing him from dying in the first place! Martha had no trouble believing that Jesus could have healed Lazarus but in her mind the situation seemed totally impossible.

How often does the Lord allow circumstances to seem the most impossible before He acts! Abraham was 100 and Sarah was not only barren but past the age of child-bearing. That didn't stop God from fulfilling His promise! God deliberately led the Israelites to the shores of the Red Sea where they were seemingly trapped and about to be crushed by the greatest army of its day. But God used that occasion to demonstrate His power and glory not only to the Israelites but to all the nations who heard about what He did!

Scripture is full of "impossible" situations that only served to magnify God's glory when He acted. None is greater than raising His Son from the dead when all hell would have kept him there. If God can do that He can do anything! We limit Him by our unbelief.

Things That Are Not

Listen to Paul's words in Rom. 4:17 where Abraham's faith was spoken of as being in "the God who gives life to the dead and calls things that are not as though they were." Think about those two kinds of things. Are they not at the heart of what God's purpose is all about? Who can bring life out of death but God? And Who else can create that which does not presently exist?

When God created the stars did He look at the empty heavens, wring His hands, and say, "But what can I do? There's nothing there to work with?" God doesn't need anything to work with. He's God! He is not dismayed by the current state of the church. There are no emergency meetings in heaven to try to figure out what to do! His promises will not go unfulfilled.

1 John 3:2-3 says, "Dear friends, now we are children of God, and what we will be has not yet been made known. But we know that when he appears, we shall be like him, for we shall see him as he is. Everyone who has this hope in him purifies himself, just as he is pure." What an amazing thing to "know"!

Think about what John is saying there. He expresses the glorious hope of our being like Christ "when he appears." But he *also* directly connects that hope with something we do. "Everyone who has this hope in him purifies himself." That's something that happens now, *before* Christ comes. Remember that Abraham not only believed the promise but he also obeyed what God told him to do.

To hear some preach it, all that is really necessary is to "accept Jesus." That's it. No strings attached. Being a disciple is a good thing and you'll receive rewards but that's really optional. Just "accept Jesus," attend church services, wait for the "rapture" and, by some magic, baby Christians who can barely get along with each other down here will be suddenly transformed into mature saints who will be "like him."

If God's purpose is that His people "be conformed to the likeness of his Son" — and it is (Rom. 8:28-29) — how can that purpose be fulfilled in those who are taught to "accept Jesus" and warm a pew on Sunday? Wouldn't that be sort of like Abraham saying to God, "I accept your promise but I think I'll stay where I'm at. That part about leaving home and going to a land You'll show me later is surely optional. Besides think of all the good I can do right here?"

I don't want to over-think what John said and read into it things it doesn't say but I also don't want to ignore it. God inspired him to write it for a reason. God's purpose is not about our simply "getting in the door" and waiting for Jesus to come. He seeks our obedience to His Word. The rest is up to Him.

A Bride Made Ready

My mind often goes to Rev. 19:7 where John saw what was yet to come; "... the wedding of the Lamb has come, and his bride has made herself ready." That last statement is what stands out to me: **"his bride has made herself ready**." Think about that! That sounds like there is something for us to do in preparation for that day. We have a necessary part to play. Why was that statement put in there? Does it have any relevance for us today?

We can see Christ's part in all this in Eph. 5:25-27 where Paul writes, "Husbands, love your wives, just as Christ loved the church and gave himself up for her to make her holy, cleansing her by the washing with water through the word, and to present her to himself as a radiant church, without stain or wrinkle or any other blemish, but holy and blameless."

That sounds like a purposeful process to me. He is working towards a goal. How conscious are we of this goal? Are we engaged in faith and doing our part? Do we really believe such a thing can be? Will those two scriptures find fulfillment?

Unity

John 17:20-23 records part of Jesus' prayer for his disciples shortly before he went to the cross. He said, "My prayer is not for them alone. I pray also for those who will believe in me through their message, that all of them may be one, Father, just as you are in me and I am in you. May they also be in us so that the world may believe that you have sent me. I have given them the glory that you gave me, that they may be one as we are one: I in them and you in me. May they be brought to complete unity to let the world know that you sent me and have loved them even as you have loved me."

Do you believe that when Jesus prayed it was according to the will of God? Surely it was. What about this prayer? Was it some pipe dream, a nice-sounding but totally unrealistic ideal? Was the church after Pentecost the entire fulfillment of his prayer? Jesus prayed that "they be **brought** to complete unity." Doesn't that sound like a situation in which unity doesn't exist and then God brings it about? The church at Pentecost was in perfect unity from the beginning. And the unity for which Jesus prayed was "to let the world know...." That has to be something that happens here, in the world. Think about it.

The Fullness of Christ

Earlier we spoke of God's desire that the **body** of Christ become fully mature even as Jesus Christ the Head is. When that happens the entirety of "Christ" will become complete and ready for eternity.

Paul speaks of this in Eph. 4:11-13 — "It was he who gave some to be apostles, some to be prophets, some to be evangelists, and some to be pastors and teachers, to prepare God's people for works of service, so that the body of Christ may be built up until we all reach unity in the faith and in the knowledge of the Son of God and become mature, attaining to the whole measure of the fullness of Christ."

There is no way to read this and honestly contend that we play no part in this. Paul goes on to say in verses 14-16, "Then we will no longer be infants, tossed back and forth by the waves, and blown here and there by every wind of teaching and by the cunning and craftiness of men in their deceitful scheming. Instead, speaking the truth in love, we will in all things grow up into him who is the Head, that is, Christ. From him the whole body, joined and held together by every supporting ligament, grows and builds itself up in love, as each part does its work."

Again — are these empty words, an unrealistic dream, or does God intend to bring about their fulfillment?

Taking Hold

Consider Paul's words in Phil. 3:10-14 — "I want to know Christ and the power of his resurrection and the fellowship of sharing in his sufferings, becoming like him in his death, and so, somehow, to attain to the resurrection from the dead. Not that I have already obtained all this, or have already been made perfect, but I press on to take hold of that for which Christ Jesus took hold of me. Brothers, I do not consider myself yet to have taken hold of it. But one thing I do: Forgetting what is behind and straining toward what is ahead, I press on toward the goal to win the prize for which God has called me heavenward in Christ Jesus."

That's a pretty good picture of someone who has not only caught a vision of God's purpose but who is totally engaged in fully laying hold of God's promises.

The Laodicean Church

Is not the slumbering, compromised state of much of the modern church world a symptom of widespread deception? I can remember hearing a lot of preaching comparing the Laodicean church of Rev. 3:14-22 with the modern "liberal" church, the folks that deny miracles and the inspiration of scripture and preach a "social gospel." As God is my witness I am convinced that the Laodicean church describes most of the so-called evangelical world of today.

It is asleep and deceived as to its true state. It thinks it is spiritually "rich" and needs nothing (or at least nothing all that serious) and has no clue just how "wretched, pitiful, poor, blind and naked" it is. Its outward prosperity and apparent success has blinded it to reality. Laodicea was a city of relative prosperity and it bred an atmosphere that put the church there to sleep. Sounds familiar, doesn't it! What will God do to awaken His people?

Stopping Short

We have been so immersed in the spirit of the world that we have been deceived into stopping short of God's purpose and promises. God promised the Israelites the land of Canaan but a whole generation failed to enter in. Did the promise fail? Of course not! They failed to enter in because of their unbelief. Heb. 3:19.

Near the end of the 40 years of wandering in the wilderness the Israelites had conquered some territory east of the Jordan River and many had settled there. The temptation was to stop there and say, "That's good enough. We have a nice place to live. Conquering walled cities and giants is not realistic."

Is it any different with us? Have we laid claim to the inheritance for which Christ died or have we simply declared much of it to be unattainable? Of course it IS unattainable through our own efforts as was conquering the land for the Israelites but what about the promises of God? I'm afraid that, unlike Abraham, we do a lot of "staggering" at the promises.

Chapter 12

A Radiant Church

Bro. C. Parker Thomas, the founder of Midnight Cry Ministries, was a man of vision, a vision that extended far beyond the religion of his day. A number of times in his public ministry Bro. Thomas shared the following quote from A.W. Tozer:

> "Surely we need a baptism of clear seeing if we are to escape the fate of Israel (and of every other religious body in history that forsook God). If not the greatest need, then surely one of the greatest is for the appearance of Christian leaders with prophetic vision. We desperately need seers who can see through the mist. Unless they come soon, it will be too late for this generation. And if they do come, we will no doubt crucify a few of them in the name of our worldly orthodoxy. But the cross is always the harbinger of the resurrection."

> "Mere evangelism is not our present need. Evangelism does no more than extend religion, of whatever kind it may be. It gains acceptance

for religion among larger numbers of people without giving much thought to the quality of that religion. The tragedy is that present-day evangelism accepts the degenerate form of Christianity now current as the very religion of the apostles and busies itself with making converts to it with no questions asked. And all the time we are moving farther and farther from the New Testament pattern."

"We must have a new reformation. There must come a violent break with that irresponsible, amusement-mad, paganized pseudo-religion which passes today for the faith of Christ and which is being spread all over the world by unspiritual men employing unscriptural methods to achieve their ends."

Dr. Tozer graduated to glory in 1963. If what he wrote was true in his day — and it was — how much more do his words apply in our day? Is this condition not a fruit of deception? Have we not been exhorted to "contend for the faith that was once for all entrusted to the saints"? Jude 3. And yet on we plunge, each one contending instead for his particular religious "brand," imprisoned by walls of tradition — or worse, compromising with modern culture for the sake of numbers and the appearance of success.

It would no doubt shock us to know how few adherents of so-called Christian churches in our day are even converted. It would also shock us were we able to observe the church as she was in the beginning side-by-side with what passes for the church today.

The True Church

Of course I am keenly aware that the church as God sees it and the church as men see it are very different things. Only those who have been truly converted, born of God's Spirit, are truly part of His church. And He "knows those who are His." 2 Timothy 2:19. God's focus is upon them.

And so while in one way we may well lament and decry the widespread apostasy we see around us, yet it is well to remember that none of this has taken the Lord by surprise. He is not dismayed. Everything is proceeding as He has foreseen and He remains firmly in control, the end sure.

There is a parallel between conditions today and conditions when Jesus came to Israel. The nation as a whole was in a terrible apostasy, far from God, all the while retaining a militantly held outward form of godliness. Yet among the nation there was a true remnant that awaited the fulfillment of God's promises through the prophets. It was to them that Jesus was sent. In the eyes of men the nation as a whole was seen as "Israel" but in God's heart and mind "Israel" referred only to that remnant. It was not about Abraham's *physical* descendants but about the *spiritual* ones. See Rom. 9, particularly verses 6-8, and John 8:39. In process of time great judgment fell upon the nation — but the true remnant was saved. And God didn't look to any scheme of man to make that happen.

The Day of Jesus Christ

Today, I believe we are drawing nearer and nearer to the end of the age and the grand climax of God's plan regarding this present evil world. Satan is loose as never before, actively deceiving and destroying those who harden their hearts to truth. Yet it is in the midst of earth's darkest hour that God will finish His work. And He will take the very climate of darkness that envelopes and destroys the lost to purge, purify, and prepare His elect for the glorious day when Christ returns.

Paul wrote in Phil. 1:6, "being confident of this, that he who began a good work in you will carry it on to completion until the day of Christ Jesus." Years ago that verse jumped out at me. Paul saw the "big picture." He didn't speak merely of a work that would be carried out **until they died**. He spoke of work that would continue until **the day of Christ Jesus**. He looked far beyond his own day to that glorious climax of history at the coming of Christ. Though the Philippian believers to whom Paul penned those words died long ago and went to be with the Lord, there is in some sense a work that continues in them even today!

Paul wrote of that day in Eph. 1:9-10 where he said, "And he made known to us the mystery of his will according to his good pleasure, which he purposed in Christ, to be put into effect when the times will have reached their fulfillment — to bring all things in heaven and on earth together under one head, even Christ."

He Will Do It

1 Thessalonians 5 warns that the day of the Lord will come suddenly and unexpectedly upon the world and none of them will escape. It is in that context that he encourages the believers to be "alert and self-controlled" (verse 6), to "encourage one another" (verse 11), together with many other exhortations.

Then in verses 23-24 he says, "May God himself, the God of peace, sanctify you through and through. May your whole spirit, soul and body be kept blameless at the coming of our Lord Jesus Christ. The one who calls you is faithful and he will do it." What a glorious promise! But notice in particular the connection with the Lord's coming. That is the very point when everything comes together, the climax of the work God has promised to complete.

How can such a thing be? Because "The one who calls you is faithful and he will do it"! We have a part to play but ultimately it is because we serve a "God who gives life to the dead and calls things that are not as though they were." Rom. 4:17.

Through the prophets God promised a Savior. Through the apostles He promised to complete the resulting salvation in a people from every tribe, tongue and nation, gathering them eternally to Himself in one amazing display of His power and glory. He fulfilled the earlier promises. He will also fulfill the latter ones.

A Radiant Church

My mind goes once again to the glorious picture Paul paints in Eph. 5:25-27 — "Husbands, love your wives, just as Christ loved the church and gave himself up for her to make her holy, cleansing her by the washing with water through the word, and to present her to himself as a radiant church, without stain or wrinkle or any other blemish, but holy and blameless."

In this passage Paul relates the total love commitment Christ has made to bring the church to "radiance" to the marriage relationship between a man and a woman. The marriage relationship as God intended it is compared in a number of ways with that of Christ and the church. In marriage two become "one flesh" (Gen. 2:24). Christ and the church are likewise "one flesh." 1 Corinthians 6:15.

As we have said before we are literally part of him. He is not complete without us. Do you think Christ is content to have overcome and to be seated in glory and not bring "the rest of him" to the same glory? In speaking of husbands Paul says, "He who loves his wife loves himself. After all, no one ever hated his own body, but he feeds and cares for it, just as Christ does the church— for we are members of his body." Eph. 5:28-30. In loving the Church, Christ loves himself. We can be sure that he will do whatever it takes. The full resources of heaven are engaged and his church will be ready for that great day.

Separation Time

Jesus gave us a glimpse of the role of heaven at the end of the age in the preparation of his people for that day. In Matt. 13:24-30 we find the parable of the wheat and the tares — or the wheat and the weeds as some modern translations have it:

"The kingdom of heaven is like a man who sowed good seed in his field. But while everyone was sleeping, his enemy came and sowed weeds among the wheat, and went away. When the wheat sprouted and formed heads, then the weeds also appeared. The owner's servants came to him and said, 'Sir, didn't you sow good seed in your field? Where then did the weeds come from?' 'An enemy did this,' he replied.

"The servants asked him, 'Do you want us to go and pull them up?' 'No,' he answered, 'because while you are pulling the weeds, you may root up the wheat with them. Let both grow together until the harvest. At that time I will tell the harvesters: First collect the weeds and tie them in bundles to be burned; then gather the wheat and bring it into my barn.'"

The Harvest

Obviously our Lord understood that there would be true and false Christians all mixed together in the world. And yet when the owner's servants in the parable wanted to do something about the weeds the instruction was, "Let both grow together until the harvest."

Think of the simple lessons implied in his words. This mixture of true and false has been something permitted in the providence of God. It is not the place of men to "straighten this out." I think you would agree that this doesn't imply that carelessness and compromise are OK, simply that until a certain time, even where men of God pray and preach the anointed message of God, there will still be "weeds" among the "wheat." Were there not unbelievers who followed even Jesus at times?

But his words *also* speak of a "harvest," a time of separation at the end. The "owner" will instruct the harvesters to collect the weeds, bind them in bundles in preparation for the fire, and to gather the wheat into the barn. But who are these harvesters? The disciples didn't know either! In verse 36 they asked Jesus to explain the parable. Matt. 13:37-43 gives us his explanation:

"The one who sowed the good seed is the Son of Man. The field is the world, and the good seed stands for the sons of the kingdom. The weeds are the sons of the evil one, and the enemy who sows them is the devil. The harvest is the end of the age, and the harvesters are angels.

"As the weeds are pulled up and burned in the fire, so it will be at the end of the age. The Son of Man will send out his angels, and they will weed out of his kingdom everything that causes sin and all who do evil. They will throw them into the fiery furnace, where there will be weeping and gnashing of teeth. Then the righteous will shine like the sun in the kingdom of their Father. He who has ears, let him hear."

God has reserved the job of harvesting for angels. I'm glad He has. I'd hate to see the kind of job any of us would do! But what a promise of cleansing and purification we are given! And what a result! "The righteous will shine like the sun in the kingdom of their Father"! Only a divine effort could accomplish such a thing.

Do you believe it will happen? I do. Everything about this sin-cursed world including prevailing conditions in the professing church rises up to say it will never happen. But when a God Who cannot lie tells us something it is wise to believe it.

First Collect the Weeds

One point in Jesus' parable is worthy of special note and it concerns the weeds. Did you happen to notice the order in the instructions to the harvesters? They were told to "**First collect the weeds and tie them in bundles to be burned;** *then* gather the wheat and bring it into my barn." Regardless of what is involved in harvesting the wheat the first order of business is to deal with the weeds, separating them from the wheat.

Have you ever wondered about those bundles? What is it that would cause false believers not only to be "collected" in "bundles" but also to be "tied" and made ready for the fire? Is it not deception? What happens when men refuse to walk in light they have? Does not darkness come upon them causing them not to know where they are going? John 12:35.

In Matthew 15 we find the Pharisees offended when Jesus had told them that their worship was vain, nothing but rules made up by men. The disciples told Jesus about the Pharisees' reaction and in verses 13-14 we read, "He replied, 'Every plant that my heavenly Father has not planted will be pulled up by the roots. Leave them; they are blind guides. If a blind man leads a blind man, both will fall into a pit.'" If the Father didn't plant them who did?

Powerful Delusion

Remember the sober warning about deception just prior to the coming of the Lord in 2 Thess. 2:10-12 — "They perish because they refused to love the truth and so be saved. For this reason God sends them a powerful delusion so that they will believe the lie and so that all will be condemned who have not believed the truth but have delighted in wickedness." Once again we see the role of heaven in the process. Even as the righteous are being readied for glory those who harden their hearts to truth are given over to the darkness they have chosen and made ready for judgment. And it's not just "delusion" but rather a "powerful" delusion. What a fearful condition is being described here: to be absolutely sure you are right yet to be totally wrong and headed for the fire.

Out of the Dragon's Mouth

Remember the picture in Rev. 12:15-16 of the "dragon" spewing water out of his mouth like a flood to overtake "the woman" (God's people). But it is the "earth" that opens her mouth and drinks up that flood. In symbolic language the Lord is portraying the efforts of Satan to deceive. Notice that the "flood" comes from his **mouth**. That represents deceit in all of its forms. Remember it is out of the **heart** that the mouth speaks (Luke 6:45). Whatever comes out of his mouth comes straight from his evil heart.

And anything coming from Satan will appeal in some fashion to natural sinful men. It will appeal to the old nature and so the "earth," representing natural men, drinks up the flood. Is that not a picture of the very essence of satanic deception? How else would he approach someone if not through their sinful nature?

And I am persuaded that Satan's most successful deception is **religious** because while it appeals to the old nature it nonetheless **appears** under the guise of truth and righteousness. Remember those "bundles"? Are not many of those bundles religious? Do you see the picture? Men reject truth. God sends them a powerful delusion. The result is that they are sealed in that delusion — together with multitudes in a similar state. They are "tied" in bundles and don't know it nor are they aware of their fate.

Does this not describe much that we see in the world of professing Christianity in our day? And yet isn't it amazing that **widespread deception is actually part of the process** by which God completes the work in His people by bringing about a separation! The truth is that **everything** that happens at the end of the age, far from being a problem to God's plan, is in reality a means to a glorious end for His people.

Religious Expectations

We discussed earlier the widespread idea that a carnal divided church will suddenly vanish into thin air in a so-called "secret rapture." Christ indeed is coming, but his coming will be a sudden, shocking, and open event to a satanically deceived world. Every eye will see him. And when he comes his church will have been made ready.

But there are other expectations that some have regarding what is to come. One category that needs to be mentioned is that of "triumphalism." That term is used in a number of senses but I am referring to a variety of beliefs among professing Christians regarding the end of the age. Another term often heard is "dominion."

There are those who see as I do the errors of expecting God to rapture the church in its current condition. But they go to another extreme expecting some form of "triumph," that is, one that alters the course of events here in **this** world. Some go so far as to believe in a special company of "overcomers" who will essentially take over the world, driving the devil out and turning this world into the kingdom of God.

But the kingdom of God is not about this present world — and never will be. I believe in a triumphant church — one that will stand in the coming storm and be used of God as He finishes His work of gathering the elect from the four corners of the earth. It will be a people who shine with the glory of God in the face of the greatest darkness the world has ever known. Every effort Satan mounts to destroy the church will only serve to purify and strengthen it. The real conflict is between Satan and Christ — and Christ will triumph — and his bride will be ready for his coming.

Not Before the Rebellion

One passage that bears on both secret rapturism and triumphalism is 2 Thess. 2:1-12, the passage in which the warning of powerful delusion occurs. **Please note that this passage is specifically about "the coming of our Lord Jesus Christ and our being gathered to him**." In verse 3 Paul says, "Don't let anyone deceive you in any way, for **that day will not come until the rebellion occurs** and the man of lawlessness is revealed, the man doomed to destruction." That statement alone indicates that believers will be here and not whisked off before any real trouble starts.

But Paul continues by speaking of "the secret power of lawlessness," already at work in his day but under restraint. The "rebellion" from verse 3 coincides with the removal of the restraint upon that power of lawlessness. The result in verse 8 is that "the lawless one will be revealed." Verses 9-10 tell us, "The coming of the lawless one will be in accordance with the work of Satan displayed in all kinds of counterfeit miracles, signs and wonders, and in every sort of evil that deceives those who are perishing."

But when does this end — and how? Verse 8 says, "And then the lawless one will be revealed, whom the Lord Jesus will overthrow with the breath of his mouth and destroy by the splendor of his coming." Thus in one passage we see the age ending with a climax of Satanic power that is ultimately destroyed by the coming of Christ. That is the same coming believers await. Some, at least, will be here. I'm sure glad that the Lord has promised to be with us to the end of the age! Matt. 28:20.

Chapter one of 2 Thessalonians confirms this picture. In verse 4 Paul commends the believers for their "perseverance and faith in all the persecutions and trials you are enduring." But note **when** it is that all this ends and God makes everything right.

2 Thess. 1:6-10 — "God is just: He will pay back trouble to those who trouble you and give relief to you who are troubled, and to us as well. This will happen when the Lord Jesus is revealed from heaven in blazing fire with his powerful angels. He will punish those who do not know God and do not obey the gospel of our Lord Jesus. They will be punished with everlasting destruction and shut out from the presence of the Lord and from the majesty of his power on the day he comes to be glorified in his holy people and to be marveled at among all those who have believed. This includes you, because you believed our testimony to you." Both relief and judgment come in one glorious event, the coming again of our Lord.

Noah and Lot

The coming of our Lord is compared to both the days of Noah and the days of Lot. Luke 17:26-29. In both cases they were rescued **as the wicked were destroyed**. Neither Noah nor Lot "triumphed" by transforming the world of their today into a kingdom of righteousness. But they **did** triumph by rejecting the world and availing themselves of a divinely provided escape.

There is nothing Satan fears more than the coming of Christ because he knows full well that it signals his end. He is angry and will do everything in his power to destroy the church and banish the very name of Jesus from this earth. Not only will he utterly fail but God will even use his efforts in fulfilling all of His great promises to bring every one of His elect to glory in the end.

Romans 8

That is what Romans 8 is about. Every believer has drawn comfort from Rom. 8:28 — "And we know that in all things God works for the good of those who love him, who have been called according to his purpose." But this wonderful scripture is not just an isolated truth. While its truth is surely applicable in every age it is most particularly part of a passage that concerns the completion of God's purpose at the end of this world. But to whom does this promise apply?

Rom. 8:1-11 tells us that being God's child is not a matter of keeping His laws through some form of religious self-effort but of being indwelt by God's Spirit. Verse 9 makes it clear that if someone does not have the Spirit of Christ, "he does not belong to Christ." No compromise. No middle ground. Life or death. Heaven or hell. The destiny of all men hinges on this one simple truth. See 1 John 5:12.

Sharing Christ's Glory

God's children are called to live by the Spirit and not according to the sinful nature. Verse 17 speaks of their destiny: "Now if we are children, then we are heirs — heirs of God and co-heirs with Christ, if indeed we share in his sufferings in order that we may also share in his glory."

How great is that glory? Verse 18 says, "I consider that our present sufferings are not worth comparing with the glory that will be revealed in us." That is what all creation awaits. When God's work in us is finished then creation itself will be set free from its bondage to corruption. The curse will be forever gone! Rev. 22:3.

Specifically the hope that is spoken of is "the redemption of our bodies." Verse 23. This is the same message we find in Phil. 3:20-21 — "But our citizenship is in heaven. And we eagerly await a Savior from there, the Lord Jesus Christ, who, by the power that enables him to bring everything under his control, will transform our lowly bodies so that they will be like his glorious body." And as we "wait patiently" the Spirit helps us pray according to the will of God. Verse 25-27.

God's Purpose

This is where verse 28 comes in! It concerns God at work fulfilling His purpose in His own. And what is that purpose? Verse 29 tells us: "For those God foreknew he also predestined to be conformed to the likeness of his Son, that he might be the firstborn among many brothers." What an amazing purpose!

God has one Son yet seeks many, every one like the first! In His sovereignty He has predestined that result. The word "conformed" speaks not only of the result but also of the process that leads to that result. The "all things" of verse 28 refers to the **tools** God uses in that conforming process. Under God's mighty and loving hand every "son" (referring to men and women born of His Spirit) will become like Jesus who will then take his place forever among his brothers, always the eldest and firstborn. The end result is noted in 1 Cor. 15:28 — "… the Son himself will be made subject to him who put everything under him, so that God may be all in all." Together we will serve Him in a world where all is new and incorruptible.

Remember 1 John 3:2 where John writes, "… when he appears, we shall be like him." Hebrews 2 has some wonderful confirmations of the truths of Romans 8. Verse 10 speaks of God "bringing many sons to glory." Verse 11 says that "Jesus is not ashamed to call them brothers." Verse 17 says, "… he had to be made like his brothers in every way, in order that he might become a merciful and faithful high priest in service to God, and that he might make atonement for the sins of the people." What a glorious truth! Jesus was made like us so that we might be made like him!

How Certain is This?

Rom. 8:30 not only lists the steps leading to this end but describes every one of them in the past tense — as if they have already happened! He is God. He can do that! "And those he predestined, he also called; those he called, he also justified; those he justified, he also glorified."

Again, that is what Romans 8 is about, the glorification of God's sons. Think of some of the visions of Christ in glory. Isaiah saw him high and lifted up on a throne in radiant purity. The disciples saw him shining like the sun on the mountain top. Have you ever tried to look at the sun? Don't! Human eyes are far too frail to behold such brightness.

John saw him in a vision in Revelation 1 and was so overcome by the sight that he fell down as though dead. From our present point of view it is hard to imagine ourselves as such glorious beings but that is God's promise. Col. 3:4 says, "When Christ, who is your life, appears, then you also will appear with him in glory."

Paul continues in Rom. 8:31-32 — "What, then, shall we say in response to this? If God is for us, who can be against us? He who did not spare his own Son, but gave him up for us all — how will he not also, along with him, graciously give us all things?" Indeed!

God's Tool Box

In the rest of chapter 8 we find several of the "all things" listed. Each is something Satan uses as a weapon against us but in every case God uses Satan's weapons as His tools! Try as he will, Satan cannot win!

Victory Over Condemnation

Perhaps Satan's most universal tool in attempting to defeat Christians is that of condemnation. After all we are far from perfect. And so in verses 33-34 Paul says, "Who will bring any charge against those whom God has chosen? It is God who justifies. Who is he that condemns? Christ Jesus, who died — more than that, who was raised to life — is at the right hand of God and is also interceding for us." Remember that Rom. 8 begins, "Therefore, there is now no condemnation for those who are in Christ Jesus...."

Some of our most difficult spiritual battles concern our own spiritual weaknesses and failures. How easily do they rob us of our confidence toward God and our courage to move forward. And we all know how quickly Satan jumps in with every doubtful, negative thought he can come up with. *And yet God allows him to do so!* There must be a reason. Somehow even our shortcomings must play a part in His purpose. After all, verse 28 says He works in "all things." But how?

Well, for one thing, failure is humbling. How often do we become careless and sort of "coast" spiritually, supposing that we are strong and can handle things. Sometimes the most loving thing God can do for us is to let us fall in the mud spiritually to remind us how it really is. For God to save any of us He has to strip away all of our *self*-confidence, our prideful *self*-reliance and call us back to the cross.

At least part of His design when we fall short is that we experience a fresh revelation of Christ and the blood he shed for us that God might declare every one of His children righteous. Legally, Satan has no grounds whatever for condemnation but until we learn to stand firm upon God's perfect provision for our sin through Christ he uses our failures to hinder and discourage us.

The Fight of Faith

In 1 Tim. 6:12 Paul wrote, "Fight the good fight of the faith. Take hold of the eternal life to which you were called when you made your good confession in the presence of many witnesses." Notice that "eternal life" is something to which Timothy "was called." And yet he was exhorted to "fight" to "take hold" of it.

And so are we. One thing we often experience in the process of being conformed to Christ is failure. It is IN such times that we must fight to lay hold of God's promise of forgiveness and cleansing. 1 John 1:9. We learn to rely upon the Spirit's power and not our own strength. We experience God's love and faithfulness and the reality of Christ's intercession for us.

We discover the ugly things we all have deep inside, things we often don't even know are there, and we have opportunity to bring those very things to the cross for cleansing and deliverance. Self dies a little and the new life God has put inside us grows stronger. God works not "in spite" of our weaknesses but IN them.

Other Tools

But there are other tools in God's tool box. They include the list Paul gives us in verse 35 — "Who shall separate us from the love of Christ? Shall trouble or hardship or persecution or famine or nakedness or danger or sword?" These are examples of the kinds of external pressures Satan brings to bear upon God's children in this world. Paul's readers were all too familiar with such things. They describe the experience of many who chose to follow Christ in his day.

And it is no different in many parts of the world in our day. Typically when Satan mounts a frontal assault on the Church through persecution it has a purifying effect. False believers are eliminated and true believers are driven to ever deeper reliance upon God. But the glorious truth is that none of these things can separate us from Christ's love.

Why?

But what part do they play? Why not simply believe in Jesus and go on to heaven? Paul answers such questions by quoting from Psalm 44:22 — "For your sake we face death all day long; we are considered as sheep to be slaughtered."

That sounds terrible but it is actually wonderful! The path to glory involves suffering (Rom. 8:17). In order to experience the life to which we have been called we must die, that is, the self life to which we were once enslaved must be put to death. In one sense that was accomplished at the cross but in a practical sense it is worked in us during our life in this world. We have no idea of the depth of our need in this area but God does. And He is faithful to work in us through the "all things" He ordains for each of us.

He transforms us by the renewing of our minds as Paul tells us in Rom. 12:2. He leads us in paths of humbling, dependence, repentance, "letting go," surrender, and trust that we might experience more and more of the riches of His salvation and become more like our Lord. And He can accomplish more than we can ask — or even imagine — because what He does is based, not upon any ability in us, but upon His own power at work "within us." Eph. 1:18-21, 3:20.

What About the End?

But so far these wonderful truths have applied throughout church history and not just to the end. God has always been at work in His people with the ultimate goal in mind. What special relevance does all this have for the end of the age?

Think about the kind of world we are told to expect. Satan is allowed to unite the world under his leadership. Will he not attempt to destroy the church and blot out the very name of Christ?

Daniel the prophet was shown many things, even things concerning the end, yet told to shut up the words until that time. But one thing we do find are these words in Dan. 12:10 — "Many will be purified, made spotless and refined, but the wicked will continue to be wicked. None of the wicked will understand, but those who are wise will understand."

I can envision God doing a very special work under very special conditions. It shouldn't be hard to imagine the ranks of the martyrs being swelled as many saints lay down their lives by the grace of God in the face of Satan's onslaught. It's happening right now in some parts of the world. What will it be like as his dominion increases throughout the world?

Those Who are Still Alive

And yet we know that some at least will be here when Jesus comes. In 1 Thess. 4:15 Paul refers to those "who are still alive, who are left till the coming of the Lord." I can also envision the Lord using the climax of Satan's dominion to complete the preparation of such ones for his coming. God's grace and God's grace alone will enable every one of his children to endure whatever comes and to be ready for that day.

Now I can just hear someone saying, "Oh, you believe in sinless perfection" — or something similar. I simply believe, "… that when he appears, we shall be like him…." 1 John 3:2. Right before that John wrote, "… what we will be has not yet been made known…." If John didn't know I certainly don't! I refuse to try to figure out details that God hasn't revealed.

What's wrong with simply believing what He says and trusting Him with those details? That's what Abraham did. I'm sure there were many things he didn't understand — and wasn't shown. But he didn't demand that God satisfy his finite intellect concerning every skeptical question that came to his mind. It was enough that God had spoken. Abraham believed God. Do we?

It is God's business as to who is here when Christ comes and who goes by way of the grave but the glorious truth is that it all comes out right in the end. We are not given these truths to produce fear but rather anticipation. Never forget Paul's answer to the question as to whether any of the "things" he lists can separate us from Christ.

In Rom. 8:37-39 he writes, "No, in all these things we are more than conquerors through him who loved us. For I am convinced that neither death nor life, neither angels nor demons, neither the present nor the future, nor any powers, neither height nor depth, nor anything else in all creation, will be able to separate us from the love of God that is in Christ Jesus our Lord."

Chapter 13

Christ is All

We have been writing about deception and how to recognize it. Our approach has not been to attempt a "catalog" of specific deceptions but rather their characteristics. If we know the characteristics of deception we can more readily detect it regardless of the particular form it may take.

However, even that is not really enough. A mere list of the characteristics of deception can itself become a kind of "catalog" that we rely on to keep us safe. It is not that simple. In our zeal to judge rightly it is far too easy for us to set at naught a genuine but imperfect brother and yet to receive something or someone that seems genuine but isn't. The truth is that we are simply no match for the devil's power to deceive. It doesn't matter how smart we are or how sincere. We are in way over our heads.

The devil has been in the deceiving business a long time. All of us were born into Adam's family, a family that by nature lives under the dominion of Satan's lies. As long as we live in these bodies a part of us will naturally be susceptible to those lies in one form or another.

This age will end with deception at an unprecedented level, the entire world of lost men having been given over to "the lie." 2 Thess. 2:11. Those who stand will stand against a flood tide of darkness by which Satan hopes to destroy them. How, then, can anyone stand in such an hour? Will religious institutions and creeds save us? Religious leaders? Programs? Traditions?

Truth in Contrast

In identifying the characteristics of deception we have sought to set forth God's truth by way of contrast. The point has been made that God has not given us a religion to practice but a PERSON. That person is the Lord Jesus Christ. In every area our need is simply Christ. Christianity without Christ is just religion.

Christ is our Head. Christ is our message. Christ is our life. Regardless of what area one considers, Christ is God's answer and provision for us. And yet even if we are sound doctrinally in these matters that is still not enough. We simply must have the living presence of Christ himself.

Speaking of the church, Paul wrote in Col. 1:25-27 — "I have become its servant by the commission God gave me to present to you the word of God in its fullness — the mystery that has been kept hidden for ages and generations, but is now disclosed to the saints. To them God has chosen to make known among the Gentiles the glorious riches of this mystery, which is Christ in you, the hope of glory."

Profound words, those. And speaking in Col. 3:11 of the oneness of those God brings together in His church he writes, "Christ is all, and is in all." Ponder those words! Let your mind dwell on them! When all is said and done Christ is not just a long list of wonderful things to us: He is ALL. Everything God has for us is in Christ — plus nothing, minus nothing.

In the context Paul had been warning the Colossian believers about any supposed wisdom or knowledge that had come from some other source. In Col. 2:8 he writes, "See to it that no one takes you captive through hollow and deceptive philosophy, which depends on human tradition and the basic principles of this world rather than on Christ."

Satan well understands the place Christ occupies and so he had sought to turn believers aside through various religious ideas which sounded good but were in reality worthless. In their case some were seeking secret spiritual knowledge from so-called angels. Others had turned to religious observances like Sabbath-keeping and dietary regulations as though such things were keys to spiritual growth and success. Not so. There is no substitute for the living presence of Christ IN US.

Consider the issue of our defense against deception. Did not our Lord say, "I am ... the truth...."? John 14:6. He is not merely a "truth-teller": He IS the truth. There is no other truth. Whatever does not come from him is simply a part of Satan's lie. It is only in the light of Christ's presence that darkness and deception are exposed.

Utter Dependence

By nature we seek to be independent. We like our religion down in "black and white" where right and wrong are neatly defined and we always know what to do and say. But God has fixed it so that we are called to a life of utter dependence. No matter how capable or experienced we think we are the truth is that we simply don't know the way to go, nor are we able to avoid Satan's traps. Our only defense is Christ in us.

Consider Jesus. Did the Father simply give His Son a creed and a general plan and turn him loose? No! Jesus lived a life of moment-by-moment dependence upon his Father. In John 5:19 he said, "I tell you the truth, the Son can do nothing by himself; he can do only what he sees his Father doing, because whatever the Father does the Son also does." That's not a declaration of mere *choice* but rather a statement regarding his *ability*. "Nothing" means **nothing!** He understood that he was *unable* to do anything apart from his Father.

In John 12 Jesus warned those who refused to heed his words. He declared that the words he spoke would judge them at the last day. Of his words he declared, "... I did not speak of my own accord, but the Father who sent me commanded me what to say and how to say it." John 12:49. Think about that! Does that describe the typical "sermon" of today?

The truth is that by nature we suffer from serious delusions of adequacy! We measure our abilities against those of others and suppose that we are capable. Not when it comes to the kingdom of God!

Why would Jesus give us the parable of the vine and branches if we possessed any abilities of our own that would enhance the kingdom of God? And don't forget the lesson of Peter's failure in denying the Lord after confidently assuring the Lord that he wouldn't. It is specially interesting that this failure occurred mere *hours* after Jesus' parable! We readily understand the complete dependence of branches upon a vine but when it comes to *our own* personal need of the Lord — not so much. As Peter learned to his great regret, sincerity and good intentions are not enough.

In John 15:5 Jesus simply said, "If a man remains in me and I in him, he will bear much fruit; apart from me you can do nothing." Consider this simple truth in connection with Paul's words about "Christ in you." Suppose a man builds a great church, preaching wonderful and even biblical sermons — but it is not literally *Christ in him* doing it all but rather his own natural ability. What has he done? According to our Lord, he has done NOTHING. Let that sink in.

The religious world is full of the zealous plans, schemes, and efforts of men. In their desire to build great religious works, impressive to men, they have turned to the wisdom and the ways of the world. In the end it will come to nothing. They build but for the fire. 1 Corinthians 3:10-15.

Most of the professing religious world will go right on, thinking they are doing God's work, only to find out when it is too late. Matt. 7:21-23. But God is concerned about His true sheep, His elect, the remnant of those who truly DO have Christ in them. The warnings of scripture should point us continually to our true source of help: Christ himself. As never before we need to apprehend that simple truth, not merely as a doctrine to profess, but as a daily reality to experience. He, and he alone, is able to bring his people through to the glory God has promised.

His Presence

Moses understood this. In Ex. 33:12-13 we read, "Moses said to the Lord, 'You have been telling me, "Lead these people," but you have not let me know whom you will send with me. You have said, "I know you by name and you have found favor with me." If you are pleased with me, teach me your ways so I may know you and continue to find favor with you. Remember that this nation is your people.'"

Verse 14 says, "The Lord replied, 'My Presence will go with you, and I will give you rest.'"

Verses 15-16 continues, "Then Moses said to him, 'If your Presence does not go with us, do not send us up from here. How will anyone know that you are pleased with me and with your people unless you go with us? What else will distinguish me and your people from all the other people on the face of the earth?'" Indeed!

The account of Israel's actual experience in the wilderness should give us hope. They did not know what to do, nor where to go. They were utterly dependent upon the presence of the Lord with them even for their daily food. They were meant to learn through this "that man does not live on bread alone but on every word that comes from the mouth of the Lord." Deut. 8:3. Of course most of a whole generation failed to learn that and perished on the way. And yet in spite of all that was wrong with Israel God remained faithful to His promise and purpose!

The Blind Led

This truth is echoed in the wonderful promise of Isa 42:16 — "I will lead the blind by ways they have not known, along unfamiliar paths I will guide them; I will turn the darkness into light before them and make the rough places smooth. These are the things I will do; I will not forsake them."

By nature we love *familiar* paths. We feel more secure, more in control. But the very nature of the kingdom into which we have been called is that we are on a journey through unfamiliar territory and God is in control. We are called to trust, obey, and follow. We are pilgrims, sojourners. Here we have no "enduring city" but rather seek one to come. We are called to "go to him outside the camp, bearing the disgrace he bore." Heb. 13:13-14.

Men are forever building religious "cities" and "camps" and attaching Christ's name to them. They build and follow traditions based on the past and far too often fail even to discern, let alone follow, the Christ that would lead them now. Most of us fall prey to the unfortunate tendency to believe that "our group," "our tradition," is basically sound and that all that is needed is to pursue what we already "know" and believe with greater dedication. Is it? Would that not merely perpetuate the religious confusion that now exists? Is God the author of that? Does any group have all the truth? Have we not been compromised by the ways and ideas of this world?

How can Baptists, Pentecostals, Calvinists, Arminians, etc., ever be brought into the unity of the faith if each one clings doggedly to his own distinctive ways and beliefs? Does God applaud us when we glory in our limited understanding of truth and use it to set at naught genuine brothers and sisters in Christ? What is His priority? Is it not that we love one another and follow Christ — even when that means walking in unfamiliar paths? If we confine ourselves to paths we have known, where will that lead? Will Christ's vision and purpose for his church be fulfilled or will following those paths continue to divide the body of Christ? Can Christ not lead us beyond what we have known? I believe he can — and will — if we are willing.

Many understandably fear that this would open the door to error, to heresy. Not necessarily. It depends upon the heart. Do you really believe that God would mislead His children who truly desire to be led aright? Will He give us a snake instead of a fish, a scorpion instead of an egg? Luke 11:9-13. Our problem is that we want to be led "aright," so long as we stay within the confines of our tradition! May God enlarge our hearts and our understanding and tear down the walls that *we* have built.

Even a superficial look at the earthly life of Jesus should make it plain that he rarely did things the same way twice. Imagine two men who each see Jesus heal a blind man. One witnesses Jesus healing him by laying his hands on the man's eyes. The other sees Jesus spit on the ground, mix up some mud, put it on the man's eyes and tell him to go wash. I can just see the seeds of two denominations! Each is sure he knows the correct way a blind man should be healed! In the meantime Jesus is probably doing it yet another way!

We are not in control and nothing we learn from the past, however profitable, is a substitute for being led and empowered by the Christ who is in us today. If we attempt to build on yesterday the cloud will move on. We need to seek the Lord as never before to grant us the grace to "follow the Lamb wherever he goes." Rev. 14:4. Anything less is a deception that leads away from Christ being the Head of the Church. Christ knows where he is going. He is the only one that can steer us through the darkness and bring us safely home.

A Balance

Paul understood this. He lived with a consciousness of the "big picture" of God's purpose yet he dealt with life moment by moment as well. He understood the balance and exhorted believers to live as he did. In Phil. 3:14 we find these familiar words: "I press on toward the goal to win the prize for which God has called me heavenward in Christ Jesus." He maintained a consciousness of the "goal" and the "prize" and, motivated by that, he "pressed on."

In verses 20-21 he expresses the believer's life perspective in contrast to that of one whose "mind is on earthly things": "But our citizenship is in heaven. And we eagerly await a Savior from there, the Lord Jesus Christ, who, by the power that enables him to bring everything under his control, will transform our lowly bodies so that they will be like his glorious body."

God's Purpose

But what was the day-to-day emphasis for Paul? Was it to preach more, work harder? Surely he did plenty of those things but "pressing on" meant much more to him than that. In Phil. 3:10-11 he writes, "I want to know Christ and the power of his resurrection and the fellowship of sharing in his sufferings, becoming like him in his death, and so, somehow, to attain to the resurrection from the dead."

Paul understood that the purpose dearest to the heart of God is the transformation of those He calls from sin-darkened sons of Adam to glorious sons of God. That is an inward work, a radical heart operation. Other things have their place but what is most important to God is that we be "conformed to the likeness of his Son." Rom. 8:29. Nothing less fulfills God's eternal purpose.

That brings it down to where we live, individually. Christ in us is all about change: sin to righteousness, death to life, bondage to freedom. Every day God will be speaking to us through His Word and orchestrating our circumstances in order to bring us to the practical experience of living by Christ's life and not the corrupted one we got from Adam.

That is the essence of the Christian life. In 2 Cor. 4:10-11 he expressed it this way: "We always carry around in our body the death of Jesus, so that the life of Jesus may also be revealed in our body. For we who are alive are always being given over to death for Jesus' sake, so that his life may be revealed in our mortal body."

Sound discouraging? Not to Paul! In verses 16-18 he says, "Therefore we do not lose heart. Though outwardly we are wasting away, yet inwardly we are being renewed day by day. For our light and momentary troubles are achieving for us an eternal glory that far outweighs them all. So we fix our eyes not on what is seen, but on what is unseen. For what is seen is temporary, but what is unseen is eternal." Although he was certainly aware of those "momentary troubles" Paul nevertheless fixed his eyes on what was to come based upon the promise of God.

"Christ in you, the hope of glory," and "Christ is all and in all" meant everything to Paul. He saw in the person of Jesus everything he would ever need to one day stand before God in glory. He saw himself as the servant — the bondslave — of Christ, his Head. Rom. 1:1. It was through union with Christ's death that it became possible to actually experience death to his own old nature. Rom. 6:3-7. It was through Christ's life within that he found the power to live for God. Gal. 2:20. And, of course, it was Christ within that gave him his hope of glory. Is it any wonder he preached no other message than "Christ and him crucified"? 1 Cor. 2:2.

Not a Private Thing

Of course Paul also saw all this not just as some private individual thing between him and God but in the context of the church, the Body of Christ. And thus every expression of the life of Christ in Paul was devoted to seeing God's purpose fulfilled in a "radiant church, without stain or wrinkle or any other blemish, but holy and blameless." Eph. 5:27. The kingdom of God is not "every man for himself." God sees us as one.

Let's look again at God's vision expressed in Eph. 4:11-16 — "It was he who gave some to be apostles, some to be prophets, some to be evangelists, and some to be pastors and teachers, to prepare God's people for works of service, so that the body of Christ may be built up until we all reach unity in the faith and in the knowledge of the Son of God and become mature, attaining to the whole measure of the fullness of Christ.

"Then we will no longer be infants, tossed back and forth by the waves, and blown here and there by every wind of teaching and by the cunning and craftiness of men in their deceitful scheming. Instead, speaking the truth in love, we will in all things grow up into him who is the Head, that is, Christ. From him the whole body, joined and held together by every supporting ligament, grows and builds itself up in love, as each part does its work."

What a rich picture! We see an order of things designed by God. We see divinely called and gifted ministries devoted — not to their own exaltation — but to bringing the body into effective, functioning order. Speaking truth is essential, but it must be spoken "in love."

We see the goal expressed: "the whole measure of the fullness of Christ." We see a built-in defense against deception. We see as well God's plan that we "grow up" "in all things" and that every member of the body is involved. Where do those members get the resources for that growth? "From him" — that is, Christ. He truly is "all."

I would pose a simple question: Have we all attained to "the whole measure of the fullness of Christ?" Then does not this order of things still apply? Is this not part of God's roadmap to the fulfillment of His purpose? Of course I do not mean to suggest that it is some kind of a "method" or "formula" that we take and attempt to apply yet does it not describe God's way of doing things?

Joshua and the Commander

There is a principle in how God does things that is wonderfully illustrated in Israel's conquest of Canaan recorded in the Book of Joshua. Moses is dead and Joshua has been commissioned and encouraged to lead the people. He sends out spies who learn of the fear the inhabitants of Jericho have of Israel. In spite of the passage of 40 years they still vividly remember how God dried up the Red Sea and destroyed Pharaoh's army. With the help of a prostitute named Rahab they return safely after promising safety for her and anyone she can get under her roof.

And so they journey to the banks of the Jordan where Joshua tells them, "Consecrate yourselves, for tomorrow the Lord will do amazing things among you." Joshua 3:5. The ark is carried ahead of them and as soon as the feet of the priests who carried it touch the water God causes the river to stop flowing so they can cross on dry ground. Imagine what the folks in Jericho thought about that!

In chapters 4 and 5 a memorial pile of stones is left as a witness to the miracle God has performed and also a renewing of the covenant with the younger generation that had been born in the wilderness. (Is there a lesson for today in that?)

In the last part of chapter 5 as they draw near to Jericho Joshua looks up and sees a man standing in front of him with a sword drawn in his hand. In verse 13 Joshua asks the man a natural question: "Are you for us or for our enemies?" It seems obvious that Joshua senses that there is something unusual — probably supernatural — about this man. If I were in Joshua's shoes I would want to know just who this was and why he was there as well!

The answer to Joshua's question is very revealing: "'Neither,' he replied, 'but as commander of the army of the Lord I have now come.'" Verse 14. Think about what he said! I'm certain that Joshua was relieved to learn that the man wasn't siding with the enemy but it must have sounded strange that he wasn't on Joshua's side either!

He had come "as commander of the army of the Lord." A third army was suddenly in the picture — a supernatural one with a supernatural commander who was there on behalf of God and His purpose. He was there to fight **God's** battle. It wasn't a matter of him being on Joshua's side; Joshua needed to be on the commander's side! He was in charge, not Joshua.

As they advanced from battle to battle Joshua learned to take his orders from God's commander in battles that were rarely fought the same way twice.

How vainly do we imagine that if we do "biblical things" in sincerity that we can expect God to be "on our side." That is not how it works. God has His own plan and His own timetable for everything. The question is not whether God is on our side but rather whether we are on His — or are we really just doing our own thing?

God has a purpose conceived in eternity and being faithfully carried out by His Commander, our Lord Jesus Christ, a purpose that will be fulfilled on the day he returns in glory. Eph. 1:3-10. God's sons will be revealed in glory and judgment will rain down upon an unprepared world. Rom. 8:18-19. 2 Thess. 1:6-10. He and He alone knows what to do as well as when and how to do it. Christ is the Commander and the armies of heaven follow him — not us! Heaven has its own agenda.

What is Our Role?

Surely it will occur to someone to wonder about our role in all this. If God is sovereign — and He is — and if we have been instructed not to attempt to engineer it — and we have — then what are we to do? Are we simply to muddle on as we are? Are we to slumber on secure in the knowledge that someday, somehow, God will do it all? What part — if any — are we to play?

As Bro. Thomas so often said, our job is to "seek God and do what He says," and not to build four walls around our traditions. I believe the "Commander" is on the job today and that he doesn't pay any attention to the walls we put up. As never before we need to simply recognize our utter need of Christ, both in us and with us. There is no substitute for this.

What if Joshua had fought a few battles under the commander and then had said, "Well, I understand what to do now so we'll just take it from here"? But isn't that the way of religion? If Jesus needed His Father to both lead him and empower him for *everything he did* how much more do we need so to walk?

Follow the Lamb

And for any generations that in the providence of God follow us they certainly don't need any more "hand-me-down" religion. They need to possess "the faith once for all entrusted to the saints" (Jude 3). They need to learn as we must how the kingdom works, how to "follow the Lamb wherever he goes."

Remember Joshua's words to the people: "Consecrate yourselves, for tomorrow the Lord will do amazing things among you." Surely they have an application to us today. God is looking for a people who are awake, aware, and committed to Him, living in expectation of the fulfillment of His wonderful promises regarding our destiny.

In 2 Cor. 6:16-7:1 Paul writes: "... we are the temple of the living God. As God has said: 'I will live with them and walk among them, and I will be their God, and they will be my people.' 'Therefore come out from them and be separate, says the Lord. Touch no unclean thing, and I will receive you.' 'I will be a Father to you, and you will be my sons and daughters, says the Lord Almighty.' Since we have these promises, dear friends, let us purify ourselves from everything that contaminates body and spirit, perfecting holiness out of reverence for God."

It is surely true that it is by God's power and will that His purpose will ultimately be fulfilled and yet Rev. 19:6-8 says, "Then I heard what sounded like a great multitude, like the roar of rushing waters and like loud peals of thunder, shouting: 'Hallelujah! For our Lord God Almighty reigns. Let us rejoice and be glad and give him glory! For the wedding of the Lamb has come, and his bride has made herself ready. Fine linen, bright and clean, was given her to wear.' (Fine linen stands for the righteous acts of the saints.)" God is in charge yet there is clearly a part we play in cooperation with His purpose. The bride will have *made herself ready*.

God Communicates

There is a pattern that is plain in the scriptures: before God acts He communicates. In Gen. 18:17-19, just prior to the judgment poured out on Sodom and Gomorrah we read, "Then the Lord said, 'Shall I hide from Abraham what I am about to do? Abraham will surely become a great and powerful nation, and all nations on earth will be blessed through him. For I have chosen him, so that he will direct his children and his household after him to keep the way of the Lord by doing what is right and just, so that the Lord will bring about for Abraham what he has promised him.'"

Those who belong to Christ are Abraham's children. May we have a seeking heart and a listening ear. God will speak to us as we have need.

We find the same thing earlier in the days of Noah. Nothing could stop the hand of judgment upon the ungodly but Noah found grace in God's eyes (Gen. 6:8). He was given a message of warning to proclaim and a job to do to prepare for what was to come. Heb. 11:7, 2 Peter 2:5. Remember that Jesus compared the time of his coming to the days of Noah. Matt. 24:37, Luke 17:26. God's people are not mere "pawns on a chessboard" mindlessly being moved about by a divine hand. We have a part to play.

Think of those who awaited Christ's first coming into the world. The nation of Israel as a whole together with the religious leaders was clueless yet there was a true remnant of those who not only believed in the coming Messiah but were actively and prayerfully awaiting his coming. All they could do was to pray and wait expectantly on God but when the time came to whom did God speak? It wasn't to the religious establishment. He spoke to people like Simeon, Anna, Mary and Joseph, Zechariah and Elizabeth and even a group of shepherds. Luke 1 and 2. He even revealed the Messiah's coming to the magi from the east! Matt. 2:1-12. I believe He longs to share His heart and His plans with those who have ears to hear and a heart to believe.

Expectant Prayer

One thing that is very much a part of all this is expectant prayer. In Daniel 9 we read that Daniel learned from the prophecies of Jeremiah that the desolations of Jerusalem were to last for 70 years. Now he *could* have simply said, "That's great! God's going to take care of everything," and simply gone about his business. But he didn't.

Dan. 9:3 tells us, "So I turned to the Lord God and pleaded with him in prayer and petition, in fasting, and in sackcloth and ashes." Verses 4-19 record his impassioned prayer of repentance imploring forgiveness and restoration.

It is significant that Daniel identified himself with his people in his prayer. He didn't say, "Those miserable sinners got what they deserved." He said things like, "**We** have sinned and done wrong," "**We** have not listened," and "**We** have rebelled." Daniel himself was a God-fearing and faithful man yet he fully identified himself with the sinfulness of his people. God honored his prayer.

No Elitism

Would praying like that be out of order in our day? There has been far too much "elitism." By elitism I mean the attitude that comes from thinking of myself and those I associate with as "those who see," not like all those blind, sleeping, carnal folk in error, but somewhere "above" them spiritually.

Christ identified himself with his body, the church, ALL of them, and so should we. I understand that so-called "Christendom" is full of lost church members but there is a true remnant as well. It is not "us" and "them." It is simply "us." We are all in this together. The body of Christ has much to repent of, much to seek.

Let those who see — or think they do — not set themselves above others but embrace every true blood-bought believer whatever label he may wear and prayerfully seek for God's revealed purposes. Christ is not a Baptist; he is not Calvinist or Arminian or Pentecostal or Catholic or Methodist or — well, any other sect, division, or category you might care to name!

A Praise in the Earth

Many of the wonderful prophecies of the Old Testament, particularly the latter part of Isaiah, look forward to the coming of Christ into the world and the eternal kingdom he was to usher in. Isaiah 62 is such a passage. It looks far beyond earthly Zion to the true Zion and heavenly Jerusalem of Heb. 12:22.

Isa. 62:6-7 says, "You who call on the Lord, give yourselves no rest, and give him no rest till he establishes Jerusalem and makes her the praise of the earth." The heavenly Jerusalem will surely be "heavenly" when it is fully assembled in heaven but that's not what this prophetic command is about. It is rather a call to relentlessly pray that Jerusalem would become the "praise of the earth."

He's not talking about the earthly city of Jerusalem in the Middle East that is "in slavery with her children." Gal. 4:25. Rather this concerns "the Jerusalem that is above." Verse 26.

Even though this heavenly Jerusalem is mostly in heaven there is portion of her that remains in this world until the coming of the Lord.

That is what we are called to pray for. Even though it is "he" who must do the establishing it is significant that believers are called upon to pray that it happen. Everything God does involves someone down here praying! That is basic to how the kingdom works. We cannot orchestrate God's plan but we can surely be "workers together with Him." 2 Cor. 6:1, KJV.

Sleep

What does deception look like when it comes to the end of the age? One word that captures it is the word "sleep" or "slumber." Anything that dulls our spiritual senses to the living presence of Christ and the unfolding purpose of God is infected with the serpent's venom sent to deceive. It may be religious or it may simply be the spirit of the world. Either way we are called to be awake and alert.

Concerning the end Paul wrote: "Now, brothers, about times and dates we do not need to write to you, for you know very well that the day of the Lord will come like a thief in the night. While people are saying, 'Peace and safety,' destruction will come on them suddenly, as labor pains on a pregnant woman, and they will not escape.

"But you, brothers, are not in darkness so that this day should surprise you like a thief. You are all sons of the light and sons of the day. We do not belong to the night or to the darkness. So then, let us not be like others, who are asleep, but let us be alert and self-controlled. For those who sleep, sleep at night, and those who get drunk, get drunk at night. But since we belong to the day, let us be self-controlled, putting on faith and love as a breastplate, and the hope of salvation as a helmet.

"For God did not appoint us to suffer wrath but to receive salvation through our Lord Jesus Christ. He died for us so that, whether we are awake or asleep, we may live together with him. Therefore encourage one another and build each other up, just as in fact you are doing." 1 Thess. 5:1-11.

The end is not about "times and dates." That is God's business. It IS, however, about being awake and "ready" as Jesus so often said. As we seek Christ, walk with him, learn of him, and draw upon his life we will be ready through his grace to stand in the growing darkness — and ready when he appears in glory!

In that hour Christ truly will be all in all. Everything outside of him will be darkness and deception. Awake, child of God. His coming is drawing near. In Christ God has provided everything we need to be a "glorious church" on that day.

Appendix

My Perspective on Bro. Thomas

My perspective on Bro. C. Parker Thomas necessarily involves my own background. In the providence of God, not only did I grow up in evangelical churches, my father was a minister. Thus I was of that dread breed known as "preacher's kids"!

In my case — and by God's grace alone — I believe that was a positive thing. My dad was a simple man of humble and genuine faith, walking faithfully in the light he had. This was demonstrated later in that he sat under Bro. Thomas's ministry for some 30 years before being called home.

As I reached the end of my high school years my path seemed to lie in the direction of full time ministry in some form. Accordingly I enrolled in a Bible College that had a rich history. There I absorbed the usual variety of Bible, Theology, and ministry-related courses, an education designed to equip me to minister in the religious environment in which I had been raised.

I distinctly remember a growing spiritual hunger during those years. "There must be more than this. Why are the churches of today so different from those in the New Testament?" This hunger was stirred every time I heard someone preach with a real anointing or when I read of powerful revivals in other places and times. In all of this I sought on the one hand to be open to things beyond my past spiritual experience and yet on the other to remain firmly anchored to the Word of God. I'm very thankful as I look back that the Lord so faithfully steered an ignorant young man through the minefields of religious deception so prevalent in our day.

Following the years of schooling my path led to pastoral ministry — about 50 miles from the Bible Tabernacle! This was in the summer of 1968. I had no idea at the time of the things happening only 50 miles away.

On New Year's Eve of 1968 one of the men from our church, Bro. Jen Hartman, was invited by a co-worker to visit a church in Southern Pines, North Carolina where a great revival was taking place. This was on a Tuesday evening. The following evening we had our regular midweek meeting, held "cottage-prayer-meeting" style in our living room.

Bro. Jen's report together with copies of the Midnight Cry Messenger chronicling the visitation/revival definitely got my attention and so the following Tuesday the Hartmans and Enlows traveled to Southern Pines for the Tuesday Evening service. The atmosphere was "electric" with the Lord's presence and the people were warm and loving. Our visit only strengthened my desire to learn all I could through reading MCMs and listening to tape recordings of some of the amazing things the church had experienced in the previous year or so.

Naturally my interest included a desire to meet the man God had used in the establishment and growth of the church. At that time Bro. Thomas and several others had recently moved to Jacksonville, Florida to begin a work there. I was enjoying his words on paper and in recordings but wanted to meet the man himself.

That opportunity came one week later. We returned once again to the Tuesday Evening service and discovered that Bro. Thomas was there, back for his first return visit. The atmosphere was even more electric, the worship joyful and exuberant. I had read many accounts of the supernatural things that had been taking place and now had the opportunity to witness an example. At some point before it was time for Bro. Thomas to minister, God gave a vision to a sister in the assembly.

Bro. Thomas had been made aware that a visiting minister — me — and a group were present so he graciously took several minutes to explain what was going on. He spoke about the fact that young people had unexpectedly begun having visions going back a year or two and how they had earnestly sought the Lord about it. He related these visions to that of Peter in Acts 10:9-16 where he went into a trance and saw the vision of a large sheet full of creatures being lowered from heaven. The visions currently being experienced were like that in that the one seeing the vision would go into a trance and both see and hear the vision playing before their eyes as if it were on a movie screen. They would then come out of it and have perfect recall of what they had seen and heard and relate it to the people.

I had no trouble at all with the idea of supernatural visions. The only issue was their source. While God can certainly give visions, so can the devil. What I saw clearly in Bro. Thomas was a man who understood this and was totally committed to truth. In reality visions had been only a small part of the many amazing things the church had been experiencing. It is a major challenge to keep one's spiritual balance in the face of such things yet my witness was that Bro. Thomas had found grace to do so. He had fervently prayed about all of it with an intense commitment to stay anchored to the Word of God, testing everything by every means he knew.

Even as it had become evident that God was truly visiting the church in wonderful ways he knew not to let his spiritual guard down, enlisting the prayers of the people and counseling those used in these unusual ways to seek God and resist the devil in it all. I don't remember the particulars of the vision that evening but do recall that it "rang true." I appreciated Bro. Thomas's effort to explain these things for our benefit and had no sense whatever that they had puffed him up with pride in any way. He remained humble and focused.

I do, however, remember the message! Remember that I had been taught to prepare and deliver sermons — seeking God, of course. What I heard that evening was no prepared sermon but a mighty river from God flowing through Bro. Thomas. The subject was "Complete in Him," taken from Colossians 2:10. He simply began with a quickened thought and was borne along on that river until a great light had been shined on the completeness of the salvation we had received through Christ. It wasn't a man's ability but God's anointing that made it so.

In process of time both the Enlows and the Hartmans moved to be part of the assembly in Southern Pines and so were in a position to enjoy the Lord's ministry through Bro. Thomas on many occasions as he would visit — or when we would visit with the folks in Jacksonville. Still, I distinctly remember asking the Lord for the opportunity to sit directly under his ministry if that could be in His plan for me. And so, in 1972 my wife and I moved to Lake City, Florida about the time the Jacksonville church "migrated" there. I remember helping Bro. Thomas and Bro. John B. Campbell dig the footer for the church that was built there that summer. Later, in 1976, both Thomases and Enlows moved back to North Carolina.

As I listened to him preach throughout many years to come it became obvious that he was not stuck on any particular method as THE way to preach. If God quickened something ahead of time then he meditated on it and looked up scriptures that came to mind and often wrote down key thoughts and scriptures. Even then the "steering wheel" in his preaching remained firmly in the Lord's control as he remained free to express the Lord's present tense thoughts in his delivery. There was a genuine immediacy to the word he preached. Even when he preached on subjects he had dealt with before it remained fresh and relevant to the present need.

And yet he wasn't afraid to trust God in those times when the Lord didn't give him something in advance. I remember one particular service when he was visiting back in the old tabernacle in Southern Pines. He stood up to speak and remarked that he didn't know what he was going to preach! He began to simply make general encouraging comments.

Suddenly he paused. I was on the first row in an old building that promoted "close fellowship" so I had a good look at what was happening. There was something in his expression indicating that a distinct thought had been quickened to him. In a moment he said something like, "Well, maybe I'll comment a little." About an hour and a half later we were all sitting there with our mouths open feeling almost as if we'd had a fire hose turned on us! There was power and clarity — and revelation. No hesitation. No reaching for thoughts or what to say next. It just flowed. God was present and speaking through a yielded vessel and we had the privilege of just drinking it up.

What a difference there is between a ministry of the Spirit and a ministry of the letter (2 Cor. 3:6)! It is the difference between life and death. A ministry of the letter — typically a product of human effort in some way — no matter how sincere is powerless to impart life to the hearers. At best it only imparts biblically accurate "information" whereas those who have been born of God's Spirit can only be nourished *by* that Spirit. Bro. Thomas understood that and so consciously depended upon God. Life was imparted and God was glorified.

As I got to know Bro. Thomas over the years I came to admire many of the qualities God had so faithfully worked in Him. I would like to briefly point out a few that stuck out to me.

Bro. Thomas was a very sensitive man. As a consequence he found controversy and conflict very challenging. Every natural instinct in him would have avoided such things. Still, he was keenly aware that faithful service to God was by its very nature a warfare in the spiritual realm and that there were times and circumstances that demanded strength. And so he was led early in his ministry to specifically ask God for courage — courage to stand in battle and do the right thing. God answered his prayer. Many who saw only the courage and willingness to confront difficulties were unaware just how much grace it took but God was faithful.

And there were many challenges over the years as Satan sought by every means to attack and undermine the ministry God had committed to him. It was common for people to join us with great enthusiasm — for a time — then become offended and leave. A number of times men rose up against him in the spirit of Korah (Numbers 16:1-3). He endured seasons of criticism, slander, attempts to divide, not to mention "ministries" coming through with their pet revelations. Through it all he was enabled to keep his balance with grace and humility.

One thing that particularly blessed me was that he remained open to greater light, never supposing that he "had it all." So many think that they are protected from error by building rigid walls around their current understanding and tradition. But what about the fellow down the street who is just as rigid in his tradition? Each thinks he is right and the other one is wrong! The reality is that we need the Lord to open His Word to us and deliver us from traditions that stop short of truth and separate us from Him who IS the truth!

One is surely vulnerable to deception who carelessly runs after every new thing but there is a blessed place where we can remain open and yet diligently weigh everything by the Word and by the Spirit. That is what I observed in Bro. Thomas.

I clearly remember a Sunday in Lake City back in the mid 70s when Bro. Thomas broke some "new ground." A doctrinal issue (it isn't important which one) came to his attention and rather than rejecting it out of hand he sought the Lord and looked into the Word for a period of time. Finally the day came when he felt the freedom to share it with us.

Well! I found what he said very interesting but not convincing. A number of questions arose in my mind that hadn't been answered. I remember discussing the matter over dinner with my father who had become a part of the work by that time. The truth is that he was probably more open than I! What blesses me as I think back to that time is that Bro. Thomas simply shared his heart and let the Lord bear witness as He would. I never felt pressured to conform or to blindly embrace his convictions. He trusted God with such matters.

And so I just mostly put the matter "on the shelf" and committed it to God to show me. I wanted my own God-given convictions — and that's exactly what Bro. Thomas wanted for those who heard him. A few weeks later he and I had a brief conversation in his office in which he made a few almost off-hand comments on that particular issue and the Lord used something he said to turn a light on. For the next 10 or 15 minutes, as I walked over to where my wife and I lived, my mind was racing as the Lord "connected the dots" for me with scripture after scripture.

Of course it was nice to feel that I was "on the same page" as Bro. Thomas in that area but even nicer to know first-hand that he wasn't looking for blind followers! Of course he wasn't shy about sharing his convictions yet he steadfastly depended upon God to establish convictions in others.

Was he perfect? Not even close! God in His wisdom uses flawed human beings in the work of His Kingdom. It's a good thing too! You and I have a lot of flaws. How discouraging it would be to have a spiritual leader who lived in some high unattainable realm, and whose feet never seemed to touch the ground! But it is a great encouragement to see God use someone mightily yet to know that they are very human and daily in need of the same grace of God we are.

One thing I am perhaps uniquely positioned to share concerns Bro. Thomas's 85th birthday, as it turned out, his last before being called home. At the time his health had almost entirely kept him at home for many months. Nevertheless a celebration was planned for a Sunday morning in the Jacksonville church. My wife and I reside in North Carolina with the assembly in Southern Pines and so while I thought it was a fine idea I truthfully had no plans to make the trip.

I believe the Lord had other plans, however, and He laid it on the heart of Bro. Jimmy Robbins to rather pointedly ask me to come and participate. Something in me sensed that it was indeed something I should do so I consented. I don't remember the exact time frame but perhaps a couple of nights later I was awakened at around 2:30 in the morning or so, my mind racing with clear thoughts as to what I should say on the impending occasion. For something like 2 hours these thoughts were deeply impressed upon me. They were not thoughts about the past but rather about the future.

And so when the weekend arrived we headed south. I remember on Saturday afternoon sitting with Bro. Thomas and several others around a very informal feast, fellowshipping and swapping stories. Despite age and health his very down-to-earth easy-to-be-around personality showed through and we enjoyed our time there.

Sunday morning arrived and Bro. Thomas came very casually dressed and sat in an aisle seat towards the back, probably a little uncomfortable with an occasion focused on him but willing to go along with it.

Many interesting memories were recounted by family and friends as well as a representative of each of the four assemblies. It was a wonderful "look back" at the life of one of God's servants, at times humorous and yet with many examples — some in video clips — of the power of his ministry. Time passed and it came to be a little after noon. I was entirely willing to sit it out and declare the service over and go on but Bro. Jimmy would have none of it. Somehow he had a sense that God had given me something important to say. I believe he was right.

The central thought that had been impressed upon me was that while it was right and proper to honor Bro. Thomas's past ministry the real honor that we needed to bestow had to do with the future — after the Lord called him home. I recounted growing up in a denomination that had been founded long before by a real man of God and the various ways in which he had been honored.

As with so many movements a denomination had arisen to conserve and promote both his memory and his beliefs and practices. Churches had been named after him as well as a college. In process of time boundaries of doctrine and tradition had been erected that effectively walled off the movement from other genuine believers. (As a matter of fact one point in their doctrinal statement had walled *me* out and God had in part used that to bring me into this work.)

I recalled for the audience how many times Bro. Thomas had warned about this very thing and how easy it is for any work to become a monument to the past, building walls around something God may have indeed done — but in the process shutting out further light. All you have to do is to look around and it should be obvious that no one has all the light there is! I recalled how often we had heard Bro. Thomas quote Prov. 4:18 which says, "But the path of the just is as the shining light, that shineth more and more unto the perfect day." (KJV).

As I said earlier, I had seen him demonstrate his own openness to greater light. It is not that we go beyond the Bible but rather that we truly understand what is in it, particularly as the Lord reveals it in ways that are relevant to God's purpose at the time and to our need. The Israelites had God's promises regarding the land, yet still needed not only the Lord's presence with them but real instruction about how to cross the Jordan, conquer Jericho, etc. We too need that same presence of our Head, Jesus Christ, to walk with us and shine the light on the truth in the Word that we need at any given time. Often that involves deeper understanding than we have had before that time.

The Lord had given me the illustration of a relay race. In a typical relay race there are four runners who share the distance, each one running his or her particular "leg" of the overall race. In many ways the kingdom of God is like that. Each God-given ministry is intended by God to serve their generation, be called home, and leave the following generation to carry on. But carry on what?

The first runner in a relay race carries a wooden stick called a "baton" which must be handed off to the second runner within a prescribed space — and so on. How foolish it would be to treat the race as if the first leg were the whole race and then to build a monument or a museum to the great race that had been run, perhaps with photos, stories, video clips, and even with the baton itself on display!

And yet that is pretty much what has happened in many religious movements. How easily do they become mere monuments to the past and in so doing reject the present tense leadership of the only Head of the Church, Jesus Christ. Another common saying of Bro. Thomas over the years summed up very simply what is needed: "Seek God and do what He says."

Another possible course of action after a founder has passed on would be to relegate the past to the past and simply start a new race with a different vision totally disconnected from what has gone before. That isn't right either! In a relay race if the second runner fails to secure the baton according to the rules the entire team is disqualified. The race we are part of isn't run within the span of one lifetime. It needs to stay connected and yet move forward.

I pointed out that if the Lord tarried there would be areas where we could expect the Lord to give greater light than we had known and we would need to walk in that light. By the same token if my generation passes off the scene the same would hold true for the generation to follow. Failure in this area is why movements die spiritually. It truly isn't about any of US but about HIM and His purpose.

How often had we all heard Bro. Thomas emphasize the truth in Isa. 42:16 — "And I will bring the blind by a way that they knew not; I will lead them in paths that they have not known: I will make darkness light before them, and crooked things straight. These things will I do unto them, and not forsake them."

I said toward the end of my remarks that I could think of no greater dishonor that we could do to Bro. Thomas than to fall into the very traps he had so often warned us of and somehow seek to preserve a movement that looked back to him and his ministry. On the other hand I could think of no greater honor that we could bestow upon him than to move ahead in the same spirit in which he had walked, looking to Christ the Head, and walking in the light He gives us until that day He returns, however short or long a time that may be.

Had I waited to say such things after Bro. Thomas had been called home there might well have been many negative reactions. Such is our nature. Most of us are "settlers" by nature when God's kingdom calls us to live as "pilgrims."

But God had ordered the occasion. I hadn't even planned to go. Then God woke me up and very clearly and forcefully impressed these thoughts on my heart and mind. But the real key to what God had in mind is that Bro. Thomas was there to hear them!

Those sitting near him bore clear witness that he was in agreement with the things I was saying, nodding his head and saying, "Amen." After the service as I paused where he sat to greet him he thanked me for the things I had said. Of course, I can't take any credit but I am very thankful that the Lord Himself was so clearly present, orchestrating events, preparing us for what was to come.

This was in April of 2004. In August, Bro. Thomas passed into the presence of the Lord. We too will follow him in our time but may we be faithful during our earthly "race" as he was. It truly is just a part of a "relay race" and we will all share in the prize on that day.

It was a great privilege to know Bro. Thomas. It is also a great privilege to do as he so often told us: "Seek God and do what He says."

CPSIA information can be obtained
at www.ICGtesting.com
Printed in the USA
BVHW040730140623
665884BV00006B/204